Master of the Rings

Susan Ang

WIZARD BOOKS (UK)

TOTEM BOOKS (USA)

ART INSTITUTE OF ATLANTA LIBRARY
6600 PEACHTREE DUNWOODY RD.
100 EMBASSY ROW
ATLANTA, GA 30328

Master of the Rings

Susan Ang

with illustrations by
Enrique Melatoni

Published in the UK in 2002
by Wizard Books, an imprint of
Icon Books Ltd., Grange Road,
Duxford, Cambridge CB2 4QF
e-mail: info@iconbooks.co.uk
www.iconbooks.co.uk

Sold in the UK, Europe, South Africa
and Asia by Faber and Faber Ltd.,
3 Queen Square, London WC1N 3AU
or their agents

Distributed in the UK, Europe,
South Africa and Asia by
Macmillan Distribution Ltd.,
Houndmills, Basingstoke RG21 6XS

Published in Australia in 2003
by Allen & Unwin Pty. Ltd.,
PO Box 8500, 83 Alexander Street,
Crows Nest, NSW 2065

Published in the USA in 2002
by Totem Books
Inquiries to: Icon Books Ltd.,
Grange Road, Duxford
Cambridge CB2 4QF, UK
e-mail: info@iconbooks.co.uk
www.iconbooks.co.uk

Distributed to the trade in the USA
by National Book Network Inc.,
4720 Boston Way, Lanham,
Maryland 20706

Distributed in Canada by
Penguin Books Canada,
10 Alcorn Avenue, Suite 300,
Toronto, Ontario M4V 3B2

ISBN 1 84046 423 2

Text copyright © 2002 Susan Ang
Illustrations copyright © 2001 Enrique Melatoni

The author has asserted her moral rights.

Illustrations originally published in *Tolkien para Principiantes,*
Era Naciente, Buenos Aires, 2001.

No part of this book may be reproduced in any form, or by any
means, without prior permission in writing from the publisher.

Typesetting: Wayzgoose

Printed and bound in the UK by
Mackays of Chatham plc

This book is not affiliated with or endorsed by the J.R.R. Tolkien
Estate or any of its publishers or licensees, New Line Cinema or
AOL Time Warner Inc. It does not imply or claim any rights to
Tolkien's characters or creations.

To
Maximillian Michael Wolff

Contents

1 ⤳ A Very Splendid Figure

J.R.R. Tolkien, author of *The Hobbit* and *The Lord of the Rings*, is perhaps the greatest fantasy writer ever to have lived; he is certainly the most influential. But there is a darker side to this great man. He is also the creator of one of the most dangerous and communicable diseases known to man: Tolkienomania. This disease can be described as follows:

Most often transmitted through reading, although it can also be communicated through other media, such as film. Symptoms: during the initial stages of the disease, patient may suffer loss of appetite and refuse to appear for meals. Eyes will be glazed. Sufferers may turn violent or experience serious anxiety attacks should the next volume not be to hand. In the later stages of the disease, the glazed look disappears, but only to be replaced by a fanatic gleam in the eye. This and the bulging pocket or rucksack – in which will be stored a copy/multiple copies of The Lord of the Rings *with which to infect others – are warnings that the disease is about to be transmitted. No known cure exists.*

Behind this light-heartedness lies a serious point. The chief characteristic of fans of *The Lord of the Rings* (the book) is a single-mindedness about the worth and wonder of the work itself. Even before the Peter Jackson film cast its spell over cinema audiences around the world ('One film to bring them all and in the darkness bind them', as Gandalf might have said), the world has been full of Tolkienomanes. In the UK in 1996, the bookshop chain Waterstones ran a poll for the Top 100 books of the century. *The Lord of the Rings* topped the poll, beating the likes of George Orwell's *Nineteen Eighty-four* and J.D. Salinger's *The Catcher in the Rye* (*The Hobbit* came nineteenth). The book itself has never been out of print since its first publication in 1954–5, and has sold over 100 million copies. And for years the world has been full of Tolkien societies, Tolkien criticism, Tolkien web-pages and women calling themselves 'Galadriel'.

The film of *The Lord of the Rings* is a very good film. It is all in glorious technicolour, gives a visual concreteness to Middle-earth, which is at one level very satisfying, and has some breathtaking moments (the Moria sequences are, in particular, quite superb). It is all very enjoyable. But the film is not the book.

What is it that makes the book so great? As Tolkien himself said, *The Lord of the Rings* is primarily an 'exciting story' (*Letters*, p. 212). That was what he thought the people who had enjoyed it had responded to and this, he said, was how it had been written. But it is not only an exciting story, or rather, it is not just because it is an exciting story that people have been reading it for nearly fifty years. So, what is it about Tolkien's work, in particular *The Lord of the Rings*, which has prompted and continues to prompt such responses? Why does it enthral, excite and perhaps above all, *move* readers? What makes it work? There are probably no short answers to these questions. But the fact that his work is read today as avidly, if not more avidly, than it was when it was first published, and has a breadth of appeal clearly shown by its translation into more than thirty-five languages, suggests that *The Lord of the Rings* deals in universals. It would not otherwise have transcended time and culture as it has.

This book is an attempt to illuminate the world of J. R. R. Tolkien, hopefully showing some of what makes 'Tolkienomania' such a contagious disease. It looks at the man himself, where he came from, what shaped his thinking and how he might have felt about the phenomenon which he created. From there, we move on to the books themselves, starting with *The Hobbit* and then looking at *The Lord of the Rings*. The books have had a massive influence, both good and bad, on fantasy as a genre since their publication. Without Tolkien, there might have been no David Eddings, Diana Wynne Jones, J.K. Rowling or *Star Wars*. Looking at this, we begin to see the more far-reaching, but no less important, aspects of Tolkien's world. Ultimately, there is the phenomenon itself in all its many forms, from websites to language-schools. At the back of the book have been included some useful sources of reference. Finally, there is a brief *Who's Who*, *Where's Where* and *What's What* of Middle-earth, as well as some historical background to the events described in *The Lord of the Rings*.

2 ～ Tolkien's Life

On 3 January 1892, John Ronald Reuel Tolkien was born in Bloemfontein, South Africa. His father, Arthur Tolkien, was English, but of German – more specifically Saxon – extraction. The Tolkiens had apparently arrived in England during the early eighteenth century. Though they appear to have been associated with the professions of clock and watch manufacturing, and also piano making, Arthur Tolkien himself, at the time of his elder son's birth, was the manager of the Bank of Africa – hence his presence in Bloemfontein, the financial capital of South Africa.

Mabel Tolkien, the baby's mother, thirteen years younger than her husband, came, like him, from Birmingham. Her maiden name had been Suffield, and it was with her family, rather than the Tolkiens, that her son would identify himself. As Tolkien would write to his own son, Michael,

Though a Tolkien by name, I am a Suffield by tastes, talents and upbringing, and any corner of that county

[Worcestershire] *(however fair or squalid) is in an indefinable way 'home' to me as no other part of the world is. (Letters*, p. 54)

Mabel had come out to Africa to marry Arthur Tolkien, but disliked the place for its landscape and climate. And when Ronald, as he came to be known to his family, was three, and his brother Hilary one, Mabel Tolkien shipped her young family back to England on a visit. Arthur Tolkien was expected to follow later.

He never did. Coming down with rheumatic fever in late 1895, Arthur Tolkien then suffered a haemorrhage from which he died. What he had left behind for his widow and sons would be difficult to live on. Mabel, for the moment continuing to live with her parents, decided that she would have to manage her sons' education herself, while looking for somewhere inexpensive to stay.

She and her sons eventually settled in Sarehole in 1896, where they were to live for the next four years. The period at Sarehole, which Tolkien was to call 'the longest seeming and most formative part of [his] life', would provide some of the inspiration for his fictions of Middle-earth. The name of the hamlet may have suggested the eventual form of Hobbit accommodation. One of its inhabitants was a farmer, nicknamed by Ronald and Hilary the 'Black Ogre', who once chased Ronald for picking mushrooms. And among the local dialect words picked up by the brothers was 'gamgee', the word for cotton wool, named after a kind of surgical tissue invented by a Birmingham doctor of that name.

Roots and unexpected branches

During this time, Mabel Tolkien began Ronald's education and, under her tutelage, he learned, among other things, the rudiments of Latin and French. Languages, and language itself, would become one of his lifelong passions. He was also introduced by his mother to a wide variety of storybooks, including *Alice's Adventures in Wonderland* (1869) and George MacDonald's 'Curdie' books (1872, 1883). Tolkien also read Andrew Lang's collections of fairy tales. This included the story of Sigurd and the dragon Fafnir, which comes from the German *Nibelungenlied*. (This also contains a ring, although Tolkien later wrote, in response to a critic's comment that the One Ring was the ring of the German tale, that 'Both rings were round, and there, the resemblance ceases' (*Letters*, p. 306).)

Each of these stories offers clues to Tolkien's later writing, although, in the light of Tolkien's comments, one should perhaps beware of reading too much into them. He seems to have had little time for 'researchers'. And his attitude to over-complex reading/interpretation may perhaps best be demonstrated in the episode where Gandalf stands at the door of Moria. Here the wizard can be found wasting a good bit of time and energy trying to work out what 'Speak, friend, and enter' requires as a password. He once knew, as he says, all the spells in all the tongues of Elves, or Men, or Orcs, that were ever used for such a purpose. He knows too much. All that is required is the speaking of the word 'friend', which had been plainly stated, not enigmatically encoded. The over-complex mind may be debarred from entry into Moria – and into the work. As Gertrude Stein might have said: 'A story is a story is a story is a story.'

With this in mind, it may be possible to observe that 'Roverandom', a story which Tolkien wrote for younger children, has something of a Lewis Carroll-like flavour to it. The opening of *Alice's Adventures in Wonderland*, with its holes and White Rabbits, suggests intriguing links with the holes and Hobbits which open Tolkien's own first published novel. The 'Curdie' books, with their goblins and tunnels, may well have provided the inspiration for the Goblins of *The Hobbit* (1937), who develop into the Orcs of *The Lord of the Rings* (1954–5).

Fafnir may have been the first dragon for Tolkien, inspiring his life-long fascination with them. His first attempt at story writing, of which few other details remain,

concerned a 'green great dragon'. However, despite the well-known assertion 'I desired dragons with a profound desire', Tolkien's dragons are all bad 'uns. Ancalagon the Black, Smaug the Golden, Glaurung the Golden, even Chrysophyllax, in the short story 'Farmer Giles of Ham', and the White Dragon of 'Roverandom', are at least unpleasant, if not downright wicked.

Tolkien began his formal education at King Edward's School in Birmingham, a school with an extremely high academic reputation, in 1899. He would continue there, except for a short interval spent at St Philip's School, when Mabel Tolkien moved to be near the Birmingham Oratory. She had become a Catholic, incurring the wrath of both the Suffields, who were strongly Protestant, and the Tolkiens, who were Baptist. Her conversion was a decision which came to influence her son's life strongly.

Riddles in the dust

At school, Ronald continued to study languages, adding Greek and German to his Latin and French, and also English literature, which was taught by a medievalist with a preference for plain English words over their fancier cousins. It was this master, Brewerton, who also introduced Tolkien to the glories of Chaucer, Middle English and, eventually, Old English. Tolkien continued to acquire languages through the years and in the process also made up his own. The languages of Middle-earth were not his only forays into linguistic creation. There were also, in his youth, 'Nevbosh' (New Nonsense) and 'Naffarin'.

It was at school, too, that he helped found the 'T.C.B.S.' (Tea Club, Barrovian Society). This was an unofficial society whose nucleus comprised Tolkien, Robert Gilson, Christopher Wiseman and George Smith. Tolkien and these friends, all senior boys, were school librarians, and the club had begun with tea sessions in the library, but developed into a society in which intellectual interests could be shared. The venue for meetings later moved from the library to the tea room in Barrow's Stores – hence the addition of 'B.S.' to the original initials 'T.C.'. It was not a literary group in the same way as the Inklings would be. But it may be seen as a precursor of sorts, providing the same kind of intelligent conversation and convivial all-male company which Tolkien found stimulating and continued to enjoy at Oxford (where he formed the Apolausticks) and even after his marriage. Meetings of the Tea Club – apart from the tea – appear to have consisted mainly of conversation about the boys' various intellectual interests, which ran from painting and music to science and mathematics. All of them were versed in Classical literature, and Tolkien added his interest in language and Germanic literature to the pot.

Window on the west

Mabel Tolkien's death from diabetes in 1904, 'hastened by the persecution of her faith' (*Letters*, p. 54), when Ronald was nearly thirteen, meant the Tolkien brothers came under the guardianship of Father Francis Morgan, the parish priest. Father Francis, while continuing to be supportive in all ways, even financially, initially sent them to stay with a widowed aunt-by-marriage, Beatrice Suffield. She, however, turned out not to be the best choice of guardian, showing them little affection or understanding, and the two boys were unhappy there. Later, Father Francis sent Ronald and Hilary to board with a Mrs Faulkner, who lived behind the Oratory, so that they could be nearer to him.

It was here that Tolkien first met the girl who later became his wife, Edith Mary Bratt. Edith was also a lodger at Mrs Faulkner's. Like Tolkien, she was an orphan, and she was three years his senior. She was pretty, engaging and musical. As Tolkien's official biographer, Humphrey Carpenter, writes: given the personalities and their position, 'romance was bound to flourish' (*J. R. R. Tolkien*, p. 48). These could possibly be summed up as 'romantic' and 'lonely', although terms such as these never really do justice to people or a situation, and can only gesture towards broad truths. A letter written by Tolkien in 1972 to his son Christopher expresses his desire to speak to someone of 'things that records do not record: the dreadful sufferings of our [Edith's and Ronald's] childhoods, from which we rescued one another, but could not wholly heal the wounds that later proved disabling ...' (*Letters*, p. 421).

This 'boy–girl affair' was hardened into something more when the relationship met with opposition. Father Francis felt that Tolkien (who was about eighteen at this time) should be working for an Oxford scholarship. Without this, he would be unable to afford to meet the fees. Tolkien was forbidden to communicate with Edith until he was 21, and

although he meticulously kept to his promise not to do so, he wrote to her on his 21st birthday to propose marriage and was accepted. We may only speculate as to the psychological roots of this emotional tenacity. Given Tolkien's record of continuous movement and early loss, that constancy may perhaps have been the expression of a desire for something stable. There was a family precedent of sorts. Mabel Suffield had been proposed to by Arthur Tolkien when only eighteen and considered too young by *her* family to be formally betrothed. They had exchanged secret letters, and only when she was 21, and Arthur had landed his managerial position with the Bank of Africa, was the engagement allowed to be formalised.

Many meetings

Between leaving King Edward's School and going up to Exeter College, Oxford, Ronald, his brother Hilary, and a number of other people went on a walking holiday in Switzerland. This was an excursion from which the mountainscapes of *The Lord of the Rings* may well have come. It was on this trip that Tolkien acquired a postcard that he kept carefully, bearing a reproduction of the German artist Madalener's *Der Berggeist* (the spirit of the mountain), showing an old man with a white beard, a long cloak and a wide-brimmed round hat. Tolkien labelled this 'Origin of Gandalf'.

At Oxford, while reading for a Classics degree, Tolkien became interested in comparative philology, which he studied under Joseph Wright. Comparative philology, roughly speaking, at that time concerned itself with how languages evolved, and how evolutions in one language might be used to understand evolutions in another. It also looked at connections between different languages and how words might have shifted, with sonal or other modifications, across languages over time and what tracing the pattern of

such affiliations might tell us. While he ended up obtaining only a Second Class in his Honours Moderations, the first major exam taken by Oxford undergraduates, his Comparative Philology paper was marked 'pure alpha'. This result pushed him into changing over from Classics to the School of English Language and Literature.

In the middle of Tolkien's undergraduate years, the First World War intervened. Most young men were signing up, motivated by patriotism as much as social pressure. Those who did not do so risked being branded cowards, and young men not in uniform might be offered a white feather, symbol of such perceived cowardice. Tolkien's situation was not an easy one. He summed it up as 'No degree: no money: fiancée' (*Letters*, p. 53). Tolkien chose to endure the censure and stayed up to finish his degree, taking a First in Finals in 1915. He then '[b]olted into the army', being assigned to the Lancashire Fusiliers, 13th Battalion, and was, the next year, married to Edith, who had meanwhile converted to Catholicism. Their first son, John, was born in 1917. There would be three more children born to them: Michael (b. 1920), Christopher (b. 1924) and Priscilla (b. 1929).

Two of the T.C.B.S. members were killed in the war: Robert Gilson and George Smith. Tolkien himself lived through the horrors of trench warfare till he

was finally hospitalised with trench fever in 1916. Through all this, he was impressed with what he saw of the British soldier, who for him came to embody certain qualities that would find their way into his conception of the Hobbits. They were stoical and, although they had little imagination, showed quiet courage in the face of apparently insurmountable odds. It was also during the war, while on sick leave, that Tolkien began setting down the first tales of *The Silmarillion* onto paper.

Among the wise

After the war, Tolkien's academic career began to take root. After the Armistice, he returned to Oxford, joining the staff of the *Oxford English Dictionary* (*New English Dictionary*) as an assistant lexicographer, meanwhile also taking on freelance tutoring in Anglo-Saxon with the University. From there, he moved on to a Readership in English Language at Leeds University, a post later converted to a Professorship. He was happy there. A letter from him to his publisher says: 'I was devoted to the University of Leeds, which was very good to me, and to the students, whom I left with regret.' (*Letters*, p. 305) When he left Leeds, with regret, in 1926, it was to return to Oxford as the Rawlinson and Bosworth

Professor of Anglo-Saxon, a post that he would hold for twenty years before being elected Merton Professor of English Language and Literature. He was, at the time of his return, thirty-five years of age.

As an academic in his own time, Tolkien was well enough thought of, although in the world of modern academia he might not have survived as happily. He tended to work slowly and meticulously, publishing a respectable body of academic material, although this would never have the currency of his fictional work. As Diana Wynne Jones, today a fantasist of stunning originality both for adults and children, and who herself was lectured to by Tolkien at Oxford, recalls: 'Oxford was very scornful of fantasy then. Everyone raised eyebrows at Lewis and Tolkien and said hastily, "But they're excellent scholars as well".' (*Official Autobiography*, http://www.leemac.freeserve.co.uk) Tolkien also appears to have been a charismatic lecturer, impassioned about his subject. The poet W. H. Auden attests to the forcefulness of his renditions of *Beowulf*. Wynne Jones's image of his lectures, as compared to C. S. Lewis's, however, is a little more wry: '... C. S. Lewis and J. R. R. Tolkien were both lecturing then, Lewis booming to crowded halls and Tolkien mumbling to me and three others.'

In the house of J. R. R. Tolkien

The family life of the Tolkiens appears to have been, on the whole, a happy one, perhaps with the minor irritations that most families experience. There are hints of the occasional difficulty between Tolkien and his wife Edith, some of which were attributable to differences over religion. Edith Tolkien appears to have been at times resentful of having been made to convert to Catholicism and the pressure on her to do things like go to confession, which she may not always have wanted to do.

Tolkien's early letters to his wife, those which have made it into print, are playfully affectionate. What Edith Tolkien meant to her husband may perhaps also be inferred from the one-word inscription that Tolkien chose for her grave after her death in 1971. The word is 'Lúthien'. It was, as Tolkien said, not a sentimental fancy. Edith had been his Lúthien – and if we may extrapolate from *The Silmarillion* what this might mean, it suggests not just a figure of grace and beauty, but an inspiration, a steadfast companion, and more.

His letters to his children, of which there are a great many more in print, including the annual Father Christmas Letters (written by him in the guise of Father Christmas), reveal him as a profoundly loving parent who was interested in his children as individuals (not just as his children). He took pains to amuse them, encouraged them in their interests (which in Christopher Tolkien's case were often his father's as well), and spoke openly to them of his own thoughts and experiences. The letters are unashamed in their expression of feeling and discussion of belief, yet manage to avoid the compromised language of easy sentimentality.

A very fine person

Tolkien's letters to his friends and even business acquaintances convey opinions upon a wide range of topics which have been thought through and considered, from politics to religion, from literature to ecological issues and the state of modern society. Perhaps his main *bête noir* was the 'machine', which he condemns in his letters, lamenting the pollution produced. He felt his house was 'racked with noise and drenched with fumes'. Tolkien saw the machine as representing the attempt to 'actualize desire, and so to create Power in this world'. *The Lord of the Rings* is imbued with a passionate love of nature and an equal distrust, if not hatred, of the Machine. Saruman's evil is demonstrated in his tree-felling and his use of those trees to feed the fires of Orthanc. This image carries with it associations of industrialisation.

Tolkien's letters furthermore show a man always courteous, often witty, with a sharp intelligence and, above all, one deeply honest and very kind. There is a letter to C.S. Lewis concerning things that Tolkien had said, or was supposed to have said, about Lewis and/or his writing, which Lewis had been hurt by and which he had written to Tolkien about (*Letters*, pp. 24–5). The letter is moving in the depth of the friendship conveyed within, in the assuagements it offers, in the honesty of the attempt to explain his own position, in the affirmations it makes.

Tolkien had met and become friends with C.S. Lewis in 1926, on his return to Oxford. They had not taken to each other at first, Lewis noting dismissively in his diary, 'No harm in him: only needs a smack or so'. They moved quickly, however, from guardedness to alliance and then to friendship. They became fellow conspirators against the 'disguised Orcs' in the Faculty of English, and also companions, fellow intellectuals and literati who would sit in Lewis's rooms on Thursday nights to discuss all manner of things. It was after a midnight conversation with Tolkien and another friend, Hugo Dyson, that Lewis shifted from his theological position as simple theist, one who believed in the existence of *a* God, but in no particular religion, to that of full-fledged Christian.

Lewis was an enthusiastic admirer of Tolkien's work, and it is possibly due to his continued encouragement and interest that *The Lord of the Rings* was written. *The Lord of the Rings* may have,

 in part, been started in response to Stanley Unwin's urging him to write 'a new *Hobbit*'. Walter Hooper, however, who was Lewis's secretary and, later, literary advisor to the Lewis estate, wrote that Tolkien had told him (Hooper) that 'he had been reading various genealogies and appendices to Lewis long before there was any written story', and quoted Tolkien as saying, 'You know Jack ... He had to have a *story*! And that story – *The Lord of the Rings* – was written to keep him quiet!' (Preface to *Of This and Other Worlds*, p. 13)

The fellowship of the Inklings

Together with Charles Williams, Tolkien and Lewis would form the nucleus of the Inklings, a society of Christian literary male *bon-vivants*. They would meet on Tuesdays in the Eagle and Child and on Thursdays in Lewis's rooms in Magdalen College. Here they would talk, read aloud to each other from their works in progress, and comment on each other's work. Even after Lewis's election to a Chair in Medieval and Renaissance Studies at Cambridge in

1954, Lewis continued to travel to Oxford weekly. Meetings of the Inklings were shifted to Mondays to accommodate his schedule. There were others who drifted occasionally into the meetings. These included Lewis's brother, Major Warren Lewis, or 'Warnie', Owen Barfield, a London solicitor, and Dr R.E. Harvard, who looked after both Lewis and the Tolkien household in his professional capacity. The group also later included Christopher Tolkien.

The Hobbit and *The Lord of the Rings* were 'midwived' by the Inklings, who heard chapters read out as they were written, and commented on them. The encouragement that the group provided was probably of immense importance. Tolkien wrote that Lewis's interest and encouragement had meant a lot to him and kept him writing in the belief that his work had more than a personal value. Apart from this, the presence of the rest of the group provided each of the Inklings with a sounding board, people against whom to test out ideas, and who were capable of providing intelligent, informed and sensitive comment.

Despite the largely happy ambience of meetings of the Inklings, there were also tensions and uneasiness, which would surface over time and which would eventually lead to an unspoken parting of ways between Tolkien and Lewis, the most prominent members of the group. Upon Lewis's death in 1963, Tolkien was to write to his son Michael,

I am sorry that I have not answered your letters sooner; but Jack Lewis's death on the 22nd has pre-occupied me. It is also involving me in some corres-pondence, as many people still regard me as one of his intimates. Alas! that ceased to be so some ten years ago. We were separated first by the sudden apparition of Charles Williams, and then by his marriage ... (Letters, p. 341)

Tolkien, while apparently enjoying at some level Charles Williams's company, had felt there to be no communion between their minds at any deep level, and his letters also claim not particularly to have liked Williams's work. Lewis, however, had been very taken with Williams when they met, and had enthusiasti-cally drawn him into the circle. Both men liked each other's work, and also shared other literary likings that excluded Tolkien.

There may have been a degree of jealousy over what Tolkien might have felt to be Williams's usurpation of his own place in Lewis's affections. There was also the rapidity with which the *Narnian Chronicles* had made their appearance, gaining Lewis even more literary kudos while Tolkien's own creation was still being slowly and painfully carved out. While Lewis had always been enthusiastic about Tolkien's work, both in private and publicly, Tolkien had not particularly liked Lewis's *Narnian Chronicles*, finding them, as he said, 'out of the range of [his] sympathy' (*Letters*, p. 352), and feeling that Lewis's secondary world was not properly thought out. Lewis's implicit – if not explicit – distaste for Catholicism may have been another wedge that eventually drove the two men apart.

Tolkien himself was a deeply committed Catholic, whose Catholicism infused all that he did. To him, Christian observances and the Sacraments were all-important; going to church, taking communion, going to confession – all these were a strong part of his existence. It would thus seem surprising that his fiction avoids any direct reference to religion, also refusing to yield up overtly Christian patterns, as Lewis's *Narnian Chronicles* do. However, Tolkien did write that *The Lord of the Rings* was a 'fundament-ally religious and Catholic work; unconsciously so at first, but consciously in the revision'. That, he said, was why he had not put in, or had cut out, 'practically all references to anything like "religion", to cults or practices, in the imaginary world'. The religious element was 'absorbed into the story and the symbolism' (*Letters*, p. 172). Tolkien's Christianity, or Catholicism, may not surface in direct reference within *The Lord of the Rings*. It is, however, patently there in the 'world-view' as implicit in the work.

There are other possible causes for their relationship souring. Lewis had married an American divorcée, Joy Davidman. Tolkien, apart from his probable views about marriage to a divorcée, did not, in any case, like Joy, who appears to have been a little pushy. Edith Tolkien did not like Lewis. (The wives, however, appear to have liked each other.) Lewis had also not bothered to inform Tolkien of his marriage. As Tolkien wrote in the letter already quoted above, he learned of it 'long after the event'. Whether this is the sum of reasons for the cooling does not matter. The friendship, sadly, *had* cooled. It had, however, while it lasted, especially during its first twenty years, been a source of much pleasure. It had also been a literary stimulation to both men who had, in their close association, helped and inspired each other in the production of works that would quickly become canonical (accepted as standard) and, in Tolkien's case, archetypal, within the genre of fantasy.

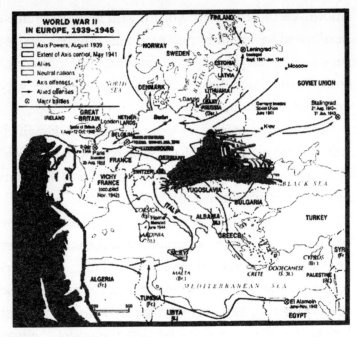

WORLD WAR II
IN EUROPE, 1939–1945

The shadow of war

Tolkien had fought in the First World War and lived through the Second. Two of his sons, Michael and Christopher, had fought in the latter. Both wars had fundamentally changed society and the individual's relation to it, redrawn world maps, and indelibly marked the consciousness of all who had lived through them. It is difficult not to read *The Lord of the Rings* through the lens of war. Tolkien, however, asserted that the main idea of his great work had *not* been a 'war product'.

As an author who gave his life to the history of

Middle-earth, Tolkien's word on these matters must be allowed to stand. However, it may still be possible to suggest that the war(s) and the work are not entirely unrelated. His feelings about the one may have influenced the other.

At the very least, the mood of the work, which was written under the shadow of the Second World War, owes something to it. There is at times a grimness, even a bleakness, a wondering-how-it-will-all-end feeling pervading the book. The gladness of the ending is the gladness of grace scant-looked-for: they are surprised by joy. The Hobbits and their quiet perseverance owe something to Tolkien's sense of those who, with him, had occupied the trenches in the First World War. Despite Tolkien's desire to sever the war from his work in the minds of others, it is also true that he drew analogies between the two. For instance, he compared the 'aeroplane of war' (which he especially loathed) to 'Nazgûl-birds' (*Letters*, p. 115), and likened the waging of the war to 'attempting to conquer Sauron with the Ring' (*Letters*, p. 78). Such sayings have not helped others to see the war and his work as detached from each other.

The Lord of the Rings changed Tolkien's life – by small degrees at first, then radically. The reviews that first greeted the publication of the work had been mixed. Some, like the oft-mentioned reviews by

Edmund Wilson and the poet Edwin Muir, had been ill-natured, attacking the work for 'childishness', its 'Boy's Own' ethos, and its over-simplified moral palette. Other criticisms, launched over the years, concerned themselves with its perceived 'escapism', its lack of interesting female figures, and so on and so forth. But there were also the enthusiasts. C.S. Lewis, who twice reviewed *The Lord of the Rings*, in 1954 when *The Fellowship of the Ring* had made its appearance, and again the following year, when the whole had been published, was, predictably, one of these. As he warned Tolkien, however, his partisanship was a two-edged sword: his own detractors, of whom there were many, would see his championship of the work as reason enough to rubbish it. W.H. Auden noted that there seemed to be no middle ground in the criticism. People either loved it or they hated it. (He was one of the former.) This is perhaps an interesting phenomenon in itself. A response to a work frequently tells us more about the reader than the work. One brings pre-existing assumptions to bear upon the reading of a work, and so, of course, 'discovers' things that confirm those assumptions. The work remains the same work, after all.

The attention paid to the work was very great, and the fan mail began to come in, perhaps bemusing Tolkien a little, but probably also pleasing him. It was, however, in the sixties that the real wave started. Ironically, this was in part due to Ace, an American publisher (today under different ownership and management). They had decided to exploit the fact that America had not yet joined the International Copyright Convention. Ace produced a cheap paperback of *The Lord of the Rings* in 1965, without having first signed any contract with Tolkien or paying him a cent in royalties. While this made Tolkien justifiably furious, it also made his work available to large numbers of people. Like *Harry Potter* before the hype started, it made its way by word of mouth. College students in particular devoured it and went to town about it: slogans such as 'Frodo lives' and Tolkien being 'hobbit-forming' were everywhere.

It became known that Ace had behaved shabbily, to put it mildly, and the lobbying for something to be done about it began. Tolkien's fans, with encouragement from him, loyally turned their backs on this volume of doubtful virtue. Robin Hobb (aka Megan Lindholm), today herself a major talent in the field, writes of her own response to that episode,

[w]*hen I discovered that those who were courteous at least to living authors would not have bought the Ace editions, I saved rigorously and purchased all four books in Houghton Mifflin hardbacks. It cost me a*

whopping $5.95 each. It took me so long to acquire the whole set that the bindings did not match. (Meditations on Middle-earth, p. 87)

Tolkien had spent much of his life having to be careful about money. Even after the publication of *The Hobbit*, which had done well, money had still been to him a source of some anxiety. A letter to Allen & Unwin about Houghton Mifflin's desire to use some of Tolkien's own illustrations for an edition of *The Hobbit* says, diffidently, that they might want to suggest to the American publisher that they offer some small consideration for the use of the pictures.

The Lord of the Rings was to change all that. Even before the increased publicity from the incident with Ace caused sales to begin their astronomic rise, Tolkien's contract with Allen & Unwin, stipulating half-profits rather than royalties, had already begun to garner amounts larger than his annual income from the University. The rise put Tolkien's *magnum opus* into the bestseller bracket and, before his death in 1973, he had become an extremely wealthy man.

After *The Lord of the Rings*, Tolkien worked sporadically on *The Silmarillion*, which publishers were now keen, in the general demand for 'more Tolkien', to bring to press. However, this kept being interrupted, by work and other things, and in the event would be published, under the editorship of his son, only after his death. Retiring in 1959, Tolkien and his wife continued to live in Oxford for a time, but eventually moved to live near Bournemouth in 1968. Edith was happy here, Tolkien perhaps less so. The society of Bournemouth threw up little in the way of grist to his intellectual mill.

When Edith died three years later, however, at the age of eighty-two, Tolkien moved back again to Oxford, to live in Merton Street as a resident honorary fellow of Merton College. His last years were laden with honours. He had been made a Fellow of the Royal Society of Literature in 1957 and now there were honorary degrees conferred on him both at home and abroad. In 1972, he was awarded the CBE, and also an honorary D.Litt. from Oxford. In the autumn of the following year, however, he was suddenly hospitalised with a bleeding gastric ulcer, and on 2 September 1973, John Ronald Reuel Tolkien, creator of Middle-earth, left the 'circles of this world to go where there is more than memory'.

3 ᔑ The Hobbit

According to Tolkien, his first story was written before his eighth birthday. 'It was about a dragon.' (*Letters*, pp. 214, 221) Unfortunately, this is all we will probably ever know. All Tolkien could recall was his mother pointing out that one could not say a 'green great dragon', but instead had to say 'a great green dragon'. This comment may have had the effect of subduing Tolkien's creative output, bringing it to a temporary halt. Instead, his attention turned to something that would remain a lifelong passion – language.

Thirty or so years later, he would begin another tale about a dragon, not green and great this time, but great and golden. This story would eventually evolve into Tolkien's first published work of fiction, *The Hobbit* (1937). *The Hobbit* recounts the adventures of Bilbo Baggins, a hobbit, whose staid and extremely comfortable existence is disrupted one afternoon by thirteen Dwarves and one wizard who whisk him off (without pocket handkerchief) to steal treasure from the dragon Smaug. In one fell swoop, Bilbo moves from respectable hobbit to impromptu burglar. The story recounting how *The Hobbit* first began to take shape is a well-known one. Tolkien scribbled the opening line, 'In a hole in the ground there lived a hobbit', on a blank sheet of paper he found when marking School Certificate examination scripts one summer. The line was written, although the author had as yet no idea of what hobbits actually were; the sentence had spontaneously written itself.

Hobbits, as they eventually emerged from the pen of their author, were (or are) a 'little people, about half our height, and smaller than the bearded dwarves'. They have curly hair, are without beards or magic, are 'inclined to be fat in the stomach' and dress in bright colours, going, meanwhile, unshod on their furry feet, which grow naturally leathery soles. Despite the extensive, and fairly human, descriptions in the book, some early reviewers still thought of hobbits as some kind of 'fairy' rabbit.

Many of the races and creatures of Middle-earth are essentially derived from the folklore and mythologies of Europe. But hobbits were Tolkien's own brainchild. They are quintessentially English in conception. This is reflected both in their characteristics and tendencies, which their creator affectionately caricatures and pokes fun at both here and in *The Lord of the Rings* (for example, their pipe-smoking, food-loving, hidebound ways) – and their names (Baggins, Bolger, Boffin, Bracegirdle, etc.). Tolkien himself explicitly spoke of the Saxon origin of hobbit names,

whereas the names of Gandalf and the Dwarves are taken from Scandinavian mythology. Hobbits were just 'rustic English people, made small in size because it reflect[ed] the generally small reach of their imagination', although not 'the small reach of their courage or latent power'.

How a Baggins had an adventure

The Hobbit, unlike its sequel, is generally thought of as primarily a book for young readers. Tolkien himself said that it was 'overtly addressed' to children. From that first unbidden sentence, it developed as a bedtime story for Tolkien's own young, and that initial audience influenced its mood, style and perhaps even, to a degree, the shape of its content. Its first – unofficial – 'reviewer' was also a child. Rayner Unwin, then the ten-year-old son of the man who later became Tolkien's publisher, was asked by his father to read and comment on the book's manuscript. His report, submitted for a shilling and blithely unshackled by conventional punctuation and spelling, carried the following endorsement:

Bilbo Baggins was a hobbit who lived in his hobbit-hole and never went for adventures, at last Gandalf the wizard and his dwarves perswaded him to go. He had a very exiting time fighting goblins and wargs, at last they got to the lonley mountain; Smaug the dragon who gawreds it is killed and after a terrific battle with the goblins he returned home – rich! This book, with the help of maps, does not need any illustrations it is good and should appeal to all children between the ages of 5 and 9.

The Hobbit is at one level an adventure tale. Rayner Unwin's report responds to that aspect of the work, emphasising the battles and the fighting. The other element, which seems to be regarded enthusiastically, is the treasure. In the course of his travels, Bilbo has to contend with various unpleasant types – such as trolls, spiders, Wargs (wolves with attitude) and Gollum, all of whom would like to vary their diet a little. And then there are the more mundane threats, such as belligerent humans and aggressive Elves, who are perhaps less motivated by gastronomic considerations, but are still difficult and awkward to deal with.

However, while Bilbo does land up in a number of

tricky – and sticky – situations, these never reach the point of being truly lethal. This is not to say that the book contains no casualties. Various members of the expedition to reclaim the treasure from Smaug, including Thorin, son of Thráin, King of Durin's Folk (the dwarf in charge) are killed in the climactic Battle of the Five Armies. The book is also satisfactorily full of dead goblins, wounded Wargs, petrified trolls, and spiders come unstuck.

For a good half of the book, however, Gandalf is a drily reassuring presence. He holds Wargs and goblins at bay with his power, rescues the Dwarves  and hobbit from the trolls by his wits, and serves as a guide through increasingly treacherous terrain with the Elves, Eagles and his skin-changing friends to provide extra aid and comfort along the way. And when Gandalf does depart to pursue some 'pressing business' away south, he leaves them, effectively, in the hands of a figure whose change from stodgy and timorous hobbit to one more heroic and battle-hardened is well under way. Bilbo is already braver, able to use his not negligible wits, and moreover the new owner of a magic ring.

On the shores of Middle-earth

The Lord of the Rings is written in a high and heroic tone. The general grimness helps reflect the current mood of Middle-earth. This also serves to highlight the nobility and greatness of heart that strive against it. But *The Hobbit* is different. The book seems conscious of the younger reader, to whom it is clearly addressed. It is a much more light-hearted piece than its epic sequel, and the voice of the author intrudes intermittently and addresses the child reader directly, sometimes archly, to share a joke, occasionally to sound a note of reassurance. The language is informal, direct and relaxed. And the playful interjections of the narrator usually occur at anxious or uneasy moments, helping to defuse tension. A good example of this may be found in the chapter 'Riddles in the Dark'. Here Bilbo has become separated from Gandalf and the Dwarves, and is wandering alone in the dark tunnels of the goblins, his heart 'all of a patter and a pitter'. The narrator observes:

Now certainly Bilbo was in what is called a tight place. But you must remember it was not quite so

tight for him as it would have been for me or for you.
(*The Hobbit*, p. 67)

This serves to dispel anxiety and leaves the child reader comforted because both the tone *and* content of the comments are unworried and reassuring. It has been argued that such instances mark a failure of style. The gripping drama is not allowed to maintain itself at full pitch. Deflating the terror by means of authorial intrusion detracts somewhat from the work's narrative power. Tolkien himself came to rue these lapses of style. As he later wrote to the poet W. H. Auden,

It was unhappily really meant, as far as I was conscious, as a 'children's story', and as I had not learned sense then, and my children were not quite old enough to correct me, it has some of the sillinesses of manner caught unthinkingly from the kind of stuff I had served to me ... I deeply regret them. So do intelligent children. (*Letters*, p. 215)

'I will do the stinging'

Some people think of *The Hobbit* as a *Bildungsroman* (literally, 'education novel'). This term is used to describe narratives whose shape or structure follows the growth and development, or even formation, of its central figure (in this case, Bilbo). It would, however, be over-simplistic – not to mention a little patronising – to treat Bilbo straightforwardly as the figure of the child growing up, as some critics have done. At the time *The Hobbit* begins, Bilbo is in fact a hobbit of fifty, slightly below middle age. Hobbits, as the author tells us in *The Lord of the Rings*, are considered adult upon the attainment of their thirty-third year.

The Hobbit is certainly a work which at one level is interested in, and that celebrates, the capacity of the individual for change and development. In *The Hobbit*, this development does not only refer to Bilbo's gradual movement towards intellectual, emotional or psychological maturity – a theme dominant in many novels (whether for adults or children) today. Here growth is concerned with the gradual awakening of the dormant imagination and the kindling of the individual's potential for greatness of heart and spirit, for nobility and heroism.

This may be seen most clearly in the way Bilbo gains physical courage. He begins the adventure a 'poor little hobbit' who shrieks and shakes 'like a melting jelly' when Thorin mentions the possibility of their not returning. He even needs to be carried by the Dwarves because of this fear. However, Bilbo grows and develops and, after he has slain the spider, he is a hobbit who 'feels like a different person, and much fiercer and bolder'. The sequence with the spiders, during which the dagger Sting is used and acquires its name, appears to act as a rite of passage for

Bilbo. It is a moment in his progress towards heroic status. This is the first time he uses his dagger, and its naming highlights further the significance of the occasion.

Plain quiet folks

Bilbo is not a 'traditional' or conventional hero, nor is he meant to be seen as one. Part of the point of the book lies in his *not* being one. Traditional heroes are not generally built along hobbit lines (short and inclined to be fat in the stomach), and if they have furry feet, it is a detail the histories appear to have left unrecorded. They do not normally rejoice in such names as 'Bilbo Baggins' – nor, for that matter, in names like 'Frodo Baggins' or 'Sam Gamgee' – since the point being made would equally apply to *The Lord of the Rings*. 'Bilbo Baggins' as a name is almost comical. It is difficult to take its owner too seriously because of it. Tolkien's hobbits have names more likely to evoke a smile (and perhaps also affection) than awe. Awe is a response kept for 'Aragorn, son of Arathorn' or 'Thorin, son of Thráin', those sonorous titles, heavy with the weight of history and inheritance.

In depicting Bilbo as a non-conventional hero, Tolkien challenges the notion of 'heroism' itself. If *The Hobbit* were merely concerned with celebrating traditional heroism, the story would probably have ended in Bilbo's heroic slaying of Smaug. Killing dragons is part of the traditional hero's job description. Perhaps that is why the dragon is dispatched by Bard, not by Bilbo. There are heroes *and* heroes: there are the doers and the endurers, the dragon-slayers and the ring-bearers. There are those for whom the trumpets sound, and there are also the reluctant, ordinary men who strive to find themselves sufficient for that which is required of them, and who sometimes succeed. Tolkien's vision of heroism is an ample and compassionate one, encompassing all of these points. It has a particular kindness for the small and simple people who strive against impossible odds.

Pity mixed with horror

The episode with the spiders does give Bilbo a degree of confidence in himself, as well as increasing the Dwarves' respect for him. But it is only one measure of his development, and is not necessarily the most important one either. While Bilbo's discovery of his own ability to deal out death certainly marks his growth in one way, his ability to refrain from doing so marks him as a hero in a greater, if more subtle, manner. This may be seen during the sequence with Gollum:

He was desperate. He must get away, out of this horrible darkness, while he had any strength left. He must fight. He must stab the foul thing, put its eyes out, kill it. It meant to kill him. No, not a fair fight. He was invisible now. Gollum had no sword. Gollum had not actually threatened to kill him, or tried to yet. And he was miserable, alone, lost. A sudden understanding, a pity mixed with horror, welled up in Bilbo's heart: a glimpse of endless unmarked days without light or hope of betterment, hard stone, cold fish, sneaking and whispering. All these thoughts passed in a flash of a second. He trembled. And then quite suddenly in another flash, as if lifted by a new strength and resolve, he leaped. (The Hobbit, pp. 82–3)

The prose of the first few sentences, with its jerky ragged rhythms, manages to suggest the panicked workings of animal instinct. This is not the mind in control, but the conscience-free surgings of adrenaline urging survival at any price. While the survival instinct

 is dominant, Gollum is an 'it', a 'thing'. However, the rhythm then eases into reflectiveness. Gollum is given a name in Bilbo's thoughts and becomes 'he', a person, whose 'otherness' and difference, even strangeness, are suddenly comprehended, the gulf between the two is momentarily erased as Bilbo knows what it is to be Gollum. There is no need to put out his eyes; Gollum's days are already lightless. And so Bilbo refrains from killing him. This is a moment of immense compassion, both in the modern meaning of the word and in its original (Latin) sense: *compassio*, 'I suffer with'.

The moment of holding back from killing is a fairly understated one. Yet it marks a change in Bilbo, the awakening of deep feeling, and is possibly therefore more significant than the killing of the spider as a moment indicative of growth. Certainly, in

the larger scheme of things, there could be no moment more significant. As Gandalf says truly, in *The Lord of the Rings*, the pity of Bilbo does in fact come to rule the fate of many. It is Gollum, preserved by pity, who does what Frodo, in the end, cannot: cause the One Ring to be unmade in the Crack of Doom.

A new strength and resolve

Equally, Bilbo's actions in respect of the Arkenstone are quietly significant in the tale of his growth/heroism. He gives it to Bard, so that Bard may bargain with Thorin for the share of the treasure which he has earned, but which has been withheld. On being asked how the Arkenstone has come into his possession, Bilbo answers,

'Oh well!' said the hobbit uncomfortably. 'It isn't exactly; but, well, I am willing to let it stand against all my claim, don't you know. I may be a burglar – or so they say: personally I never really felt like one – but I am an honest one, I hope, more or less. Anyway, I am going back now, and the dwarves can do what they like to me. I hope you will find it useful.' (*The Hobbit*, p. 251)

There is an awkwardness present here. Bilbo does not use high and heroic rhetoric. His language is simple, unpretentious and not particularly elegant, the vocabulary avoiding large abstract ideas like 'honour' or 'sacrifice', and is instead scaled down in favour of the small personal statement, such as 'personally I never really felt like one – but I am an honest one, I hope, more or less'. Yet, it is in this very discomfort that Bilbo's nobility (a word he does not use of his own actions) emerges. It is, in a strange way, proof of his sincerity; smoother speech might have sounded too glib. A new courage, that is quite different from the physical bravery which led Bilbo to charge and kill the spiders, is shown. The courage is moral and is shown in his attempt to do 'the right thing', even though he knows this will not necessarily be appreciated in all quarters. A sense of justice, courage and unassumingness are all characteristics in evidence at this point.

And back again

As well as charting Bilbo's growth, *The Hobbit* is also a tale about journeys and expanded space. Some might argue against this, saying that if Bilbo's journey begins with his venturing out of his hole – with all its connotations of smallness and narrowness – into the larger world, it does so only to take him towards another. This second 'hole' is the door in the mountain which Bilbo the burglar has to get through in order to get to Smaug's lair. And it might further be argued that the journey in the end merely leads back to the place of its beginning, as the work's subtitle, *There and Back Again*, in fact openly indicates. Bilbo's travels in fact lead to the expansion of mind and spirit which often result from such journeys. From the stodgy and unimaginative hobbit who left Bag End, Bilbo returns a creator, a writer, the author of *There and Back Again: A Hobbit's Holiday* and, as *The Lord of the Rings* will later show, a poet. His imagination has sprung to life.

Today, hobbits no longer inhabit mere holes in the ground. Since 1976, when its Second Supplement was published, they have resided comfortably within the pages of the *Oxford English Dictionary*, somewhere between 'Hobbism' and 'hobble v.'. The entry runs as follows:

hobbit

In the tales of J. R. R. Tolkien (1892–1973): one of an imaginary people, a small variety of the human race, that gave themselves this name (meaning 'hole dweller') but were called by others halflings, since they were half the height of normal men.

Also attrib. and Comb. Hence **hobbitish** a., resembling a hobbit, hobbit-like; **hobbitomane**, a devotee of hobbits; **hobbitry**, the cult of hobbits; hobbits collectively, or their qualities.

Its next-door neighbour in the *O.E.D.* is a similar-looking word: 'hobbits', which is, however, a beast of a rather different colour. This comes from the German *haubitze*, and is a variant of 'howitz' or 'howitzer', denoting a kind of small cannon. It is also, so the *Dictionary* kindly informs us, an obsolete word, no longer in use.

Hobbits (small cannon) and hobbits (hole-dwellers) have perhaps a couple of things in common, apart from the coincidence of their names. They are small versions of things. They can be fiery. But there the resemblance ends. Words or phrases do not make it into dictionaries without having been at least tacitly acknowledged to have a certain currency, have entered the bloodstream of language, have a claim to be recognised – as with 'Lilliput' – and a need to be explained because people will want to know what they mean – like 'boojum'. (Of which the *O.E.D.* rather unhappily says: 'a particularly dangerous kind of "snark"'.) (Snark: An imaginary animal.)

The 'canon-ical' (if I may be forgiven the pun) hobbit has become obsolete. The other – Tolkien's 'hobbit' – has become canonical and is not at all obsolete, being, on the contrary, very healthily alive in the imaginations and vocabularies of a rather large number of people today. That canonicity is itself demonstrated by the presence of the word in the *O.E.D.*, among whose lexicographers Tolkien himself was once numbered.

4 ∾ Travelling Hopefully . . .

A pattern of slow development may be traced across much of Tolkien's writing career. *The Hobbit* had been started, then abandoned, in 1930. It was finally completed in 1936, the year before its first publication, though it would go through further revisions and two more editions (1951, 1966) before it was done. Tolkien had begun *The Silmarillion*, his cycle of the myths and legends of Middle-earth, such as the Fall of Gondolin, as far back as 1916, while he was on sick-leave 'after surviving the Battle of the Somme' (*Letters*, p.221). Like *The Hobbit*, *The Silmarillion* also went through numerous alterations. Sadly, this did not see publication until 1977, four years after Tolkien's death.

Tolkien was a compulsive reviser. His short modern fairy tale for children, 'Roverandom', inspired by his son's toy dog, went through the same exacting process. Despite Tolkien having begun the story in 1925, it too was published only after his death. His academic writing fared no differently, the translations of the medieval poems *Pearl*, *Sir Gawain and the Green Knight* and *Sir Orfeo*, for instance, being completed only in the early 1960s, despite the earliest work having been started in the 1920s. Again, these were not published until after his death, due to the lack of an introduction, which he had put off writing.

As with these, so too with *The Lord of the Rings*. Between the publication of *The Hobbit* (1937) and *The Lord of the Rings* (1954–5) there elapsed a long interval of seventeen years. Most of this time was taken up thinking and planning the book, rather than actual writing. The intervention of the Second World War (1939–45) had brought with it additional duties at home and there were also inevitable periods of anxiety. Tolkien's second son Michael, for instance, was seriously injured and hospitalised in 1941 – which may have played some part in the delay. A letter to Sir Stanley Unwin in 1946, apologising for the non-completion of *The Lord of the Rings*, speaks generally, and a little vaguely, of 'troubles, domestic and ordinary'. Tolkien also cites illness, due to 'worry and overwork, mainly' (*Letters*, p. 117). But it is clear that there were also periods of non-activity, for which the causes are much less evident.

Loose ends and perplexities

During these seventeen years, Middle-earth and the tale of the ring continued to take shape. As was suggested earlier, Tolkien had had no idea of what hobbits actually were when the first line of *The Hobbit* had initially been written. Similarly, the larger significance of the ring picked up by Bilbo on his travels was not immediately clear to him. However, the links between *The Hobbit* and its sequel, and indeed with *The Silmarillion*, emerged and developed in the mind of the author as time went on. The Necromancer in *The Hobbit* gradually developed into Sauron. The ring, it transpired, was no mere magic bauble fished out of the waters by Gollum and cherished by him through the ages. Instead, it had become an object of ultimate power with a long, grim and terrifying history. Some of the revisions Tolkien made to *The Hobbit* were done in order to bring its narrative into line with the slowly progressing *The Lord of the Rings*. Middle-earth, its history, geography and mythology, its languages, and even the minutiae of its everyday existence, continued to grow and amass detail, gathering density as it did so.

This attention to detail is one of the most important aspects of Tolkien's writing. It bestows a solidity and believability, a total coherence and realism, upon his fictions of Middle-earth and the world they describe. Middle-earth has been imagined and thought through so thoroughly that the details have become mutually supportive, logical and inevitable consequences of each other.

The hidden kingdom

A very small but significant example of Tolkien's attention to detail may be found in Appendix D, which most editions carry at the back of *The Return of the King*, the third volume of *The Lord of the Rings*. Here he discusses at great length the calendar systems used by the various races of Middle-earth. At one point in this section Tolkien says,

It seems clear that the Eldar, in Middle-earth, who had, as Samwise remarked, more time at their disposal, reckoned in long periods, and the Quenya word yén, often translated 'year' . . . really means 144 of our years. (*Return*, p. 1080)

This is not just a case of Tolkien being extremely thorough. It is an excellent example of the cause and effect of the world of Middle-earth. The cause here is the immortality of the Elves, or Eldar. Its effect is how this immortality has shaped *their* language and conception of time. The logic would run something like this:

1. The Eldar are immortal and, consequently, the way they would think about time would be very different from the way shorter-lived species would think about time. To the mayfly, which lives only a day, for example, a day is a whole lifetime. To the Elves, who are immortal, a day is not even a ripple in the stream of time.

2. Language is a reflection of the way we think. It is also, to some extent, a reflection of the world we live in and also a world which might not exist, but which we could imagine.

3. The language of the Eldar should therefore reflect the way *they* think about time, and therefore the Quenya word *yén* is an expression of this partitioning of time into relatively long time-spans.

4. Our language contains the word 'year' (which is a shorter time-span, reflecting the relative brevity of our lives), but doesn't have the concept of 144-year units (because we don't need to think on a practical, everyday basis in 144-year terms, since we don't live that long).

5. Thus, when we translate from Quenya, our language doesn't have an exact equivalent for the Quenya word *yén*, and we are forced to adopt the nearest conceptual equivalent: 'year'.

This particular example demonstrates the kind of mutually supportive detail of Tolkien's world. Each detail bears up and affects other details, and this creates the coherent 'reality' of Middle-earth. Its existence is so complete in itself that in the end it can stand independently. It is, if you like, a world-in-itself. This minuteness of detail was the kind of thing that was slowly evolving in the seventeen years it took to bring *The Lord of the Rings* into full being.

Where the shadows lie

At the end of 1949, Tolkien had effectively completed the work (bar the inevitable revision or so). The next few years, however, were spent in publishing wrangles, which postponed further the book's arrival in the shops. Tolkien felt that *The Silmarillion* and *The Lord of the Rings* were essentially one work and wanted to see them published together. Neither Collins (who wanted to become Tolkien's publisher) nor Allen & Unwin, who in the event remained Tolkien's publisher during his lifetime, were interested in doing so. Neither publisher particularly liked

The Silmarillion. They considered it an odd book and thought it probably wouldn't sell. Another reason for their hesitation was that the Second World War had made paper very expensive and *The Lord of the Rings* by itself – never mind in conjunction with *The Silmarillion* – would already be costly to produce and might be considered too expensive by the average reader. Rayner Unwin, the long-ago child 'reviewer' of *The Hobbit*, estimated that the firm would lose £1,000 (approx. £30,000 in today's money) by publishing *The Lord of the Rings*. Despite this, his advice was to go ahead anyway, as he thought it was a great work. His business judgement was, in this instance, less acute than his literary sense. (He was wrong about the losses.)

Tolkien was at first obstinate about the matter, as well as perhaps affronted by the lack of interest in *The Silmarillion*, which was dear to him. As he had put it in a letter to Stanley Unwin back in 1937, '[t]he Silmarils are in my heart' (*Letters*, p. 26). However, nearing sixty and wishing to see *The Lord of the Rings* published, he eventually conceded the point. Tolkien also agreed to its publication in three parts, an idea he had been resistant to before. The last stage of the journey into print could now commence.

5 ∾ The Lord of the Rings

At one level, it is possible to think of *The Hobbit* as being part of the same extended narrative as *The Lord of the Rings*. The works share common characters. There are clear and obvious structural links between the two, and they take place in the same world. Yet, despite all this, and in spite of the similarity of their fairly light-hearted beginnings, *The Hobbit* and *The Lord of the Rings* are, in the end, works that are more unlike than alike.

This is not just to do with their length, the age of the audience, or even the books' style. These things must obviously be considered in any comparison between the two works, but the difference runs much deeper. It would seem safe to assume that, in occupying the same world, the two works would share the same outlook regarding the world and its workings. This, however, is not the case.

The tunnels winds on and on

The Hobbit is a work marked by a strong consciousness of space, and its limitations. It describes spatial extension and movements outward and onward. There are movements beyond the known and familiar spaces into the strange and marvellous from which one cannot return unchanged. It is intensely aware of space, showing vividly what it is to be in tight places, not just metaphorically, but literally: in tunnels, barrels and prison cells. And just as profoundly, it is aware of spaciousness, the relief of large spaces experienced after small. This, for instance, is demonstrated when Bilbo looks out from the tree in Mirkwood to see where they are and experiences a sense of freedom from the oppressiveness of the forest, and again, when he emerges from the tunnel to Smaug's lair into the open air.

While *The Hobbit* betrays a keen awareness of space, its sense of time is foreshortened, blunter, conscious mainly of the here and now. History, and the awareness of the past, have less of a part to play in Tolkien's earlier work. Occasionally, the work offers glimpses of a much deeper sense of time, as with Smaug's presence in the halls once owned by the Dwarves, Bilbo's gazing for what seems 'an age' on the treasure and Gollum's passage through 'endless unmarked days'. All of these instances acknowledge a larger conception of time and history than the main action of the novel otherwise suggests. However, these glimpses backward through the long passage of the ages are only fleeting ones.

Long, long ago

The awareness of time is one of the main differences between the two books. *The Lord of the Rings* is always and unfailingly conscious of time. It is constantly aware of time past, time passing, time to come. In *The Lord of the Rings*, actions acquire greater meaning when set against the larger backdrop of history. It resonates with events both in the near and distant past, and it affects, or even produces, the future. The sense of time behind, however, is always more weighty than that of time to come; there is no getting away from the consciousness of history.

The war against Sauron, for instance, takes place against the backdrop of other wars against darkness, which have taken place in other Ages. The War of the Elves and Sauron (Second Age 1693–1701), in which Gil-galad and Elendil (Aragorn's ancestor) are slain and the Ring cut from Sauron's hand, is not the only such struggle. There are even earlier conflicts that this war echoes. There are those pursued against

Morgoth (aka Melkor), whose lieutenant Sauron is, and from whom Sauron inherits the mantle of Dark Lord. (The history of these wars is given in *The Silmarillion*.)

The tides of time

Hobbits are less weighed down by a sense of time and of the past than the other individuals and races are, at least initially. To them, current events are terrible and terrifying. But they appear to be largely unaware of these events as part of the broader picture of history.

When Pippin is crushed by a falling troll upon the opening of the Black Gate (*Return of the King*), he hears, as if from a distance, the cry 'The Eagles are coming! The Eagles are coming!' He loses consciousness thinking of Bilbo, checking himself, however, with: 'But no! That came in his tale, long long ago.' (*Return*, p. 874) This arrival of the Eagles recalls the Battle of the Five Armies in *The Hobbit*. The Eagles have played a significant part in Middle-earth's history, as is recounted in *The Silmarillion*, among other things helping to defeat the winged dragons in the

Great Battle, and also rescuing Beren and Lúthien outside Angband. Their arrival is part of a much larger pattern than Pippin realises. For him, the coming of the Eagles resonates only with the one earlier instance recorded by Bilbo, which, although he thinks of it as having happened a long, long time ago, is in fact, in terms of Middle-earth's history, a fairly recent event. This foreshortened sense of history that the hobbits have may perhaps in part be set down to the relative youth of their race/species as measured against the Ents, Elves, Dwarves, and even Men. Having been around as a race for a shorter time, they have neither seen nor been part of the events that Elrond, Treebeard or Galadriel, for example, who have lived in Middle-earth since the First Age, have witnessed. In a sense, these events are not part of hobbit history. This brevity of their lives shapes their perception of time. In Lórien, the speech of Galadriel and Celeborn is infused with phrases such as 'since the days of dawn' and 'through years uncounted'. Sam's sense of a 'terrible long time', however, is measured by how long he has been away from home.

As the narrative progresses, the hobbits' knowledge and sense of the past deepens and increases. For instance, after the cheerful vulgarity of the opening chapter, in which the main awareness of time and age is formulated in terms of birthdays and family history, the second chapter, entitled 'The Shadow of the Past', moves swiftly into what is effectively a different dimension altogether.

Here, the meaning of 'time' and 'history' suddenly changes as Gandalf's story alters Frodo's (and the reader's) perspective of these things. The ring, in Gandalf's recounting, grows to become the Ring. In the movement from lower to upper case 'r' (from 'ring' to 'Ring'), it symbolically shifts from being an object of 'ordinary' magical status to become something of immeasurably greater power and significance. It feels 'suddenly very heavy' to Frodo, almost as if it becomes a symbol of history, the weight of which he feels to be pressing down upon him.

However, despite moments such as these, during which their understanding of time and history is suddenly intensified, the impact of deep time and history on the hobbits – except perhaps Frodo the Ring-bearer – is not permanent. Merry, coming out from under the spells of the Barrow-wight, says, 'The men of Carn Dûm came on us at night, and we were worsted. Ah! The spear in my heart!' But then, clutching at his breast, he opens his eyes and says: 'What am I saying? I have been dreaming.' (*Fellowship*, p. 140) Pippin quickly throws off the experience of the Palantír. As Gandalf says: 'The memory ... will probably fade quickly. Too quickly, perhaps.' (*Towers*, p. 580)

The hobbits, then, continue for the most part to perceive, exist and act within a consciousness of time that is dominated by the present rather than the past. There is an innocence in this. This innocence is important because it enables a certain optimism, a hope and belief in the future. *Not* to be aware of how actions signify in terms of patterns stretching over millennia can be liberating in its own way, if only because it then becomes possible to act without the sense of futility which can come with knowing that these things have been done before and will need to be done again. As a phrase in Tolkien's essay 'On Fairy-Stories' goes, '... we must travel hopefully if we are to arrive' (*Tree and Leaf*, p. 45).

The shadow of the past

For those of the elder races, the awareness of the past is never really absent. For them (as perhaps for the reader), the patterns are always there to be observed; whether these patterns are to be interpreted pessimistically or optimistically is a different question. It is hard not to notice the deep melancholy that runs through *The Lord of the Rings*, a work shot through with nostalgia and loss. It laments the passing of good and beautiful things and acknowledges that victory is never final. Battles may be won, but the war is never over. The book is littered with images of mutilation and breakage. There is the shattering of Frodo's sword, Gandalf's staff, Saruman's staff, Denethor's staff, the broken horn of Gondor, Éowyn's shield (and indeed Éowyn's arm), Merry's sword, Aragorn's sword Narsil (which, however, becomes Andúril, the Sword Reforged), the bridge in Moria, the citadel of Orthanc, the gate of Gondor, ruined Osgiliath, Frodo's hand with its four fingers. An infinitude of such images exists in the work. The destruction of the One Ring (itself part of the broader theme of destruction) will bring in its wake further loss; many things of beauty will disappear from the world. As Galadriel says:

… *Lothlórien will fade, and the tides of Time will sweep it away. We must depart into the West, or dwindle to a rustic folk of dell and cave, slowly to forget and to be forgotten.* (Fellowship, p. 356)

However, even without the destruction of the Ring, the pattern of things is already tended towards decline. The Ents, eldest of all, have lost the Entwives, and there are no Entings, which suggests there is no future. Some Ents, as Treebeard says, are growing tree-ish. Mighty though Gondor still is, mighty though the Dúnedain still are, their decline from their Númenorean beginnings is patent. The kingdom of Gondor has dwindled and shrunk – at the time of the Second War of the Ring, even Osgiliath, the original capital of Gondor, has become an outpost under attack. The lifespans of the descendants of the Númenoreans have lessened. That of the royal line (originally about 210 years) has, by the time of Aragorn II ('Strider') declined to about 150 years. Lothlórien, too, although still wondrous, has already begun to fade. As Treebeard notes, *Laurelindórenan* has become Lothlórien: 'The Land of the Valley of Singing Gold' has become the 'Dreamflower'. Its name has contracted; it is shifting towards sleep and forgetfulness.

To those with overview, the patterns of history would seem to be melancholy ones. A thinning seems to be discernible on the one hand. On the other, the reiteration of events through time (e.g. the wars of Sauron, the coming of the Eagles, etc.) appears to suggest that the world may be bound into cycles of history from which one may be unable to escape.

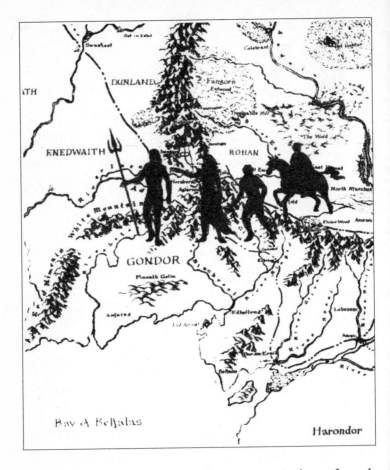

The Ring itself may stand as a reminder of such inescapable cycles. The truth is in fact more complex than this. While it may not be possible to cancel out these melancholy patterns completely, their effects may perhaps be lessened.

Not all tears are an evil

Working together with the patterns of recurrence which have seemed hopeless in their inability to be broken out of, are other patterns which are perhaps more consolatory in nature. For instance, although the battle against the Dark appears to be revisited in every age – and the War against Sauron is not the Last Battle, its victory not final but only, in a sense, a holding action – there is, nonetheless, a promise of betterment.

The original Dark Lord, Melkor, was the most favoured of the Ainur (angelic spirits) and the most powerful of them. Though Melkor, or Morgoth, as he becomes known, returns after each defeat or setback to threaten Middle-earth afresh and wreak new havoc, he is more damaged each time. By the end of the First Age, Melkor/Morgoth has burnt hands, eight great wounds, and is in constant pain. He is ultimately vanquished and flung out of Time into the Void, and Sauron, his lieutenant, takes on his master's role when this happens. But he is only one of the Maiar (the lesser Ainur). Like Melkor before him, Sauron tries to corrupt the Free People, and to dominate Middle-earth; as with his master Morgoth, however, he is wounded and weakened each time. What the pattern here suggests is that Dark Lords may continue to arise and need to be fought. However, should they be resisted, they can be damaged such that each successive incarnation of the Dark Lord returns diminished and less powerful than before.

There is another example which not only shows the pattern as both ominous and potentially consoling. This example also demonstrates the way in which Tolkien's powerful images become even more intense when seen against the patterns of history. The loss of Frodo's finger, bitten off by Gollum in his desire for the Ring, is a complex and powerful image, speaking simultaneously of many things. It speaks of loss and pain, but also a muted triumph. It is a sign of the hero who has endured (it is as 'Frodo of the Nine Fingers' that he first enters into song in Gondor). It is, however, also a sign of flaw, the absent finger an ever-present reminder of inadequacy and failure, of inability at the last moment to yield up the Ring to the fire. Neither idea – 'Frodo as hero' or 'Frodo as failure' – has more weight than the other. Both are 'truths', and together

they form a larger one: that no individual is perfect and adequate, no action finally and completely pure – indeed, no action ever fully complete. That inadequacy and incompleteness is, however, capable of redemption. This is perhaps nowhere more powerfully pointed out than in the fact that the 'redemption' – or saving – of Frodo and the completion of the quest take place at the hands of one himself inadequate and incomplete, unwilling and unaware.

In Frodo's maimed hand we may find an image which echoes and resonates with other such images: the maimed hands of Sauron, Beren and Morgoth. For Sauron's hand, too, is mutilated: from it Isildur cut the Ring in the Second Age. In the Age before that, Beren cut one of the Silmarils from Morgoth's crown; and his right hand, together with the Silmaril it held, was then bitten off and swallowed by Carcharoth the Wolf, guardian of Angband. Sam and Frodo in fact make this connection as they sit on the slopes of Mount Doom. They imagine, with slightly wistful humour, the announcement of the story of 'Nine-fingered Frodo and the Ring of Doom' and an expectant hush similar to theirs when waiting to hear the tale of 'Beren One-hand and the Great Jewel'. And to add to the tale of maimed hands, there are, of course, also Morgoth's own hands, which are burned black by the touch of the 'hallowed jewels', the

Silmarils which he has stolen. As we are told, 'black his hands remained ever after, nor was he ever free from the pain of the burning, and the anger of the pain'.

However, there is another important image of hands present in the book. In *The Return of the King*, as the epic winds towards its (provisional) conclusion, we are told that the hands of Aragorn are the hands of a healer. These hands are laid on Faramir, Éowyn and Merry, who have been hurt and lie near death. Again, the physical damage is seen in terms of a broken arm in Éowyn's case and, in Merry's, the loss of the use of the arm used to stab the Ringwraith. There is a particular compassion and power invested in this image of healing hands in the midst of images of maimed ones, the one offering potential redemption to the other.

Land of shadows

Earlier, the difference in the mood and general outlook of *The Hobbit* and *The Lord of the Rings* was mentioned. One crucial aspect of this difference lies in how the two books treat the idea of innocence and its preservation. Although the world of *The Hobbit* is a dangerous place, we may feel a general sense of protectiveness at work. Tolkien himself said that in it 'Sauron the terrible peeped over the edge' (*Letters*,

p. 26), and that 'the presence (even if only on the borders) of the terrible is ... what gives this imagined world its [appearance of truth]. A safe fairyland is untrue to all worlds.' (*Letters*, p. 24) Tolkien's own phrasing gives something away. The terrible is kept at bay in this book, at the borders, allowed only to peep over the edge, not step into it. The Shire, like A. A. Milne's Hundred Aker Wood in his *Winnie the Pooh* stories, is innocent territory, shielded from the dangers of the world outside.

The Lord of the Rings reluctantly permits the death of such innocence. Aragorn and others of the Dúnedain have striven to keep men like Barliman Butterbur and other simple folk safe, and even unaware of danger's existence. But Sauron the terrible in this work is no longer content to remain at the margins. Earlier he peeped over the edge. Now he crosses over the boundary which separates the sleepy Shire from the more troubled regions lying outside its borders. Rivendell, figured in *The Hobbit* as the 'last homely house of the West', also sheds that image of innocent domesticity, now grimly revealed as ancient fastness, citadel against the Black Riders.

When Bilbo returns home at the end of *The Hobbit*, he finds the Sackville-Bagginses about to take possession of Bag End, and a sale of effects taking place. This is no doubt upsetting, and an irritatingly unfit end (from Bilbo's point of view) for an adventure. This is, however, in the larger scheme of things, a brief and minor disruption when set against the destruction and desolation which greets the returning hobbits at the end of *The Lord of the Rings*. Even should the depredations of Saruman (aka Sharkey) and Wormtongue be halted, their effects cannot be reversed either totally or easily, as was possible in the case of Bilbo. Trees have been cut down, houses burned, hobbits killed. These are the tangible marks of experience. Past this, there is no real returning.

A sadness that was blessed

There are other indications that the world of *The Lord of the Rings* is no longer child-like or innocent. In his essay 'On Fairy-Stories', Tolkien recalls an observation of the novelist G.K. Chesterton. He had observed that the children with whom he had watched Maurice Maeterlinck's play *The Blue Bird* had

... been dissatisfied because it did not end with a Day of Judgement, and it was not revealed to the hero and the heroine that the Dog had been faithful and the Cat faithless. 'For children', he says, 'are innocent and love justice; while most of us are wicked and naturally prefer mercy'. (*Tree and Leaf*, p. 44)

The Lord of the Rings is steeped in sorrow and death and evil in a way that *The Hobbit* is not. But there also runs through it the quality of mercy. In *The Lord of the Rings*, mercy becomes more important than justice.

It is Bilbo's mercy to Gollum that ultimately allows the quest to destroy the Ring to be successfully accomplished. Nor is this true merely because it preserves Gollum past that moment. Frodo, too, will refrain in memory of that long-ago mercy, and also in remembrance of Gandalf's words:

It was Pity that stayed his hand. Pity, and Mercy: not to strike without need ... Many that live deserve death. And some that die deserve life. Can you give that to them? Then be not too eager to deal out death

in the name of justice, fearing for your own safety.
Even the wise cannot see all ends. (*Towers*, p. 601)

Justice is a force, but mercy a greater one.

Mercy, whether it is accepted or not, can also be seen in the treatment of Wormtongue and Saruman, both of whom are on the side of evil. To slay Wormtongue, as Gandalf says to Théoden, would be just. But he also observes that Wormtongue was not always as he is now, and counsels offering him a choice (in effect another chance) by which he will be judged. In Saruman's case, the mercy is even more marked. As they stand in the ruins of Orthanc, Gandalf asks Saruman, whose doings have just caused immense harm, death and destruction, whether he will not come down, join them, and take this 'last chance' of mending his ways. Saruman rejects this. On their return home, they encounter Saruman and Wormtongue again, and Galadriel extends yet another 'last chance'. This, too, is sneeringly repulsed. And when, in the ravaged Shire, Frodo faces Sharkey/Saruman for the last time, he is still pre-

pared to be merciful in the hope that, although his cure is beyond the hobbits, Saruman may still find that cure.

This mercy goes beyond mere compassion or even forgiveness. It is, ultimately, the expression of hope, a belief in the possibility of redemption and change. Many readers believe that it is because of these qualities, and the fact that the story is also exciting, that the book has stood the test of time so well.

6 ✎ After the King

'Tolkien again,' Jane sighed. 'Gollum, gollum, what has it got in its pocketses, can't these people ever be original?' The Sword of Maiden's Tears

Jane's words express the exasperation of many readers who look at fantasy after Tolkien, only to find a depressing number of pallid Tolkien lookalikes. Some of these imitations are little more than cynical attempts to write to a commercially successful 'formula'. This includes a quest, a band of companions, the battle between good and evil, many different races. Throw these together, and one can hear some authors thinking 'Swiss-bank-account-here-I-come'. Other 'imitations' stem from a mixture of slavish adoration and limited imagination in varying proportions.

However, not all works of fantasy influenced by Tolkien are derivative in the worst sense. Some are wonderful and original works in their own right, by authors with a distinct voice of their own. These authors are conscious or unconscious borrowers of types and figures created by Tolkien. Then there are other works which struggle to escape the authoritative influence of *The Lord of the Rings*, but which cannot disentangle themselves from it, and are always in the end drawn back to Tolkien's fantasy.

There are also other books which comment wittily and ironically on Tolkien and his work. They acknowledge his influence on the genre, while trying to win themselves some distance from it. An example of this last kind might be Rosemary Edghill's 'Twelve Treasures' series (unhappily incomplete), which also engages, equally wittily and ironically, with other fantasy works. The quotation above comes from *The Sword of Maiden's Tears*, the first book in the series. A line from the third book, *The Cloak of Night and*

Daggers, runs: 'Go not to the Elves for counsel, for they will say "Abort, Retry, Fail?"' Whatever it is that motivates these authors, and however great or small Tolkien's direct influence, that influence is undoubtedly there.

The golden halls

The term 'fantasy' describes works set in a world where the laws that apply to our own world are suspended, or where new – and often magical – laws may be in force. It is not that Tolkien 'created' fantasy. It existed before Tolkien, even if there was not a great deal of it around. Nearly every study that has ever tried to discuss the history of the genre in English up to 1954 has ended up wearily citing the work of Lord Dunsany (author of *The King of Elfland's Daughter* (1924)), William Morris, James Branch Cabell (creator of the imaginary land 'Poictesme'), Mervyn Peake and E.R. Eddison (who was a near-contemporary of Tolkien's, and a scholar of Old Norse). Jack Vance had also begun to write his 'Dying Earth' books. John Masefield's *The Midnight Folk* (1927) and its sequel *The Box of Delights* (1935) had been published for children. At the time *The Lord of the Rings* was published, Eddison's *The Worm Ouroboros* (1922) and his (incomplete)

Zimiamvian sequence (1935–58) were the only books with which it could be compared.

Fantasy is today a genre or type of writing with a fairly wide remit and many different sub-categories. *The Lord of the Rings*, for example, is classified as 'high' fantasy (epic in theme or scope and heroic in tone). Other examples of sub-categories include 'dark fantasy' (which some people think of as 'horror'), comic fantasy (e.g. Terry Pratchett), 'sword and sorcery', time-slip fantasy – the list could go on indefinitely. (Tolkien himself began a time-slip story, 'The Lost Road', in which his characters travel back through time to the fall of Númenor. Sadly, it was never finished.)

Fantasy was a late-developer in the literary world. It really came into being only in the nineteenth century. For some time, it continued to be so thin on the ground that it was not recognisable as a genre. *The Lord of the Rings* forced people to think about what other fantasy works already existed. It might be claiming too much to say that it was Tolkien who led to fantasy being taken seriously. But even if Tolkien was not the 'first' fantasist, he has the distinction of being the man who shaped the genre, so that now it is recognised as a separate class of work.

In his *Encyclopedia*, John Clute describes Tolkien as the 'twentieth century's single most important writer of fantasy'. As many authors have pointed out, Tolkien influenced more than just the style and form of the genre. It was the huge appeal of *The Lord of the Rings* which persuaded publishers that there was a market for fantasy. This gave the genre the boost it needed. Those publishers started looking around for writers who could give readers more of what they wanted, and the rest, as they say, is history.

Three is company

One of the ways in which *The Lord of the Rings* has had an influence on the genre is, ironically, in 'encouraging' authors and publishers to produce books in trilogies, with a gap between the publication of each volume. In some cases, this gap can be frustratingly long. This is ironic because *The Lord of the Rings* had never been conceived as a 'trilogy'. At first, Tolkien had been resistant to the idea of slicing it into three parts and publishing those parts in intervals of several months. As has already been mentioned, the publisher's reasons were to do with the high cost of paper as well as the beneficial effect they thought this might have on sales. They believed that splitting the book into three parts would spread out the costs a bit. This method of publication had certain benefits. It undoubtedly raised the level of anticipation as the public waited for the next volume to appear, but it also led to the popular misapprehension that the work was really three separate books.

Although this was an accident of publication, fantasy writers started to think in trilogies. Before the recent additions to the series, Ursula le Guin's *Earthsea* novels were firmly established as a trilogy for many years. Stephen Donaldson's 'Thomas Covenant' Chronicles – both sets – are trilogies, as is Tad Williams's *Sorrow, Memory and Thorn* sequence. Guy Gavriel Kay, the Canadian fantasist who started out as a lawyer, and who helped Christopher Tolkien to edit *The Silmarillion*, also began his writing career with a trilogy, the 'Fionavar Tapestry'. Sheri Tepper's 'True Game', 'Jinian' and 'Marianne' books are also, each of them, trilogies. There are countless others.

Today, many writers have grown more adventurous in their conception of fantasy structures. David Eddings likes the number five, Robert Jordan evidently believes that it is impossible to have too much of a good thing, and even George R.R. Martin's stunning

Song of Ice and Fire series, which started as a trilogy, is now planned as a sextet. However, the form of the trilogy is still popular. For some reason, the diptych (two volumes) has never quite caught on. Jan Siegel, an heir to the English fantasy tradition shaped by Tolkien and C.S. Lewis, has, at the time of writing, just brought out the third book of the series which began with *Prospero's Children* (1999).

'I will give you a name'

Tolkien's influence on fantasy can also be seen in the names that fantasy authors use within their works, in the details of their secondary worlds, and often in the shape of their plots. Raymond Feist, for instance, author of the 'Rift-war' books, acknowledges that 'eledhel' and 'moredhel' (elves and dark elves) are explicit 'borrowings' from Tolkien's vocabulary (edhel/eldar=elves). Donaldson's 'eoman' (twenty warriors plus a Warhaft) and 'eoward' (twenty eoman plus a Haft) are reminders of the Rohirrim name patterns and their fighting force, the 'éored'. The list of such 'tributes' to Tolkien could go on forever. But more importantly, Tolkien's heirs understood that the creation of a secondary world required consistency, a consistency which comes only with the kind of rigorous thinking at every level (language, names, concepts) that characterised Tolkien's work.

Journey to the crossroads

Many secondary worlds in modern fantasy owe something to Tolkien in their general layout and conception. Diana Wynne Jones's sly and tongue-in-cheek *Tough Guide to Fantasyland* (an A–Z of figures likely to be found in fantasy) includes several entries clearly influenced by Tolkien. Maps, which she mentions in the introduction, and which are practically compulsory in modern fantasy, are just one example. Thanks to Tolkien, quite a few fantasylands have the inevitable horse clan. In Wynne Jones's *Tough Guide*, this shows up under the entry 'Anglo-Saxon Cossacks':

Anglo-Saxon Cossacks live in the STEPPES and breed HORSES. They try to look like Horses themselves by wearing their hair in ponytails. They ride often, expertly, and acrobatically. In fact, they show off rather. Regardless of the fact that winds continually sweep the Steppes, they wear little but sleeveless VESTS and scanty TROUSERS. These people are tough. But, despite riding since early infancy, not

one Anglo-Saxon Cossack has bandy thighs. Something in their genes prevents this. They are organized normally in CLANS under a supreme chieftain but do not seem to fight among

themselves.
Nor do they fight other
peoples much. Everyone knows
better than to mess with them. If called on to fight for
GOOD, they muster eventually, but it takes time.
Oddly, since their way of life is nomadic, they live in
stone fastnesses and rarely use TENTS. ... Their
women wear long skirts and are trained to be wimps.

Secondary worlds are often populated by clans of dwarves. Elves, too, seem particularly to have gripped the popular imagination. There are, apparently, such things today as 'elf operas' (as in 'soap operas' or 'space operas') and it is all Tolkien's fault. (The film of *The Lord of the Rings* is unlikely to help matters here.)

Dark things

Fantasies are full of Dark Lords and varieties of goblins and orcs as well as kings-in-waiting and/or in exile. Then there are the wizards who can be 'distinguished by the fact that they have long beards and wear ROBES' and who can 'accompany the TOURISTS (for which read 'fellowship' or 'band of companions' – *Ed.*) as MENTORS'. Examples of wizard-mentors include David Eddings' Belgarath, Merriman Lyon in Susan Cooper's *The Dark is Rising* and Dumbledore in the *Harry Potter* books.

Nor does it stop there. The wizard who appears to die while fighting the forces of evil, but who then returns, is still popular in fantasy literature. This figure occurs, for instance, in Terry Brooks's *Sword of Shannara* (1977), one of the more obvious Tolkien imitations, and in Barbara Hambly's 'Darwath' trilogy. In Lloyd Alexander's *The Book of Three* (1966), the wizard-prince Gwydion appears to have perished in the destruction of Spiral Castle, but returns at the climax of the book. Guy Gavriel Kay puts a slight spin on this idea in his 'Fionavar' books. Here, it is not the wizard, Loren Silvercloak, who 'dies' and returns, but his power source (all wizards in Fionavar are linked to one) Matt, who is the king-in-exile of the dwarves. The figure of the Dark Lord, damaged but tiresomely on the make again, is another which keeps resurfacing – for example, Darth Vader in *Star Wars*, or Rakoth Maugrim in *The Fionavar Tapestry*.

Another more recent example of a Sauron-like Dark Lord is Lord Voldemort in J.K. Rowling's *Harry Potter* series, another British fantasy which, like Tolkien's, has become a publishing phenomenon and taken the world by storm. The series has much that is original, but there are also many obvious debts to Tolkien. Lord Voldemort, mysteriously thwarted in his attempt to kill the infant Harry, vanishes and, at the time of the first volume's opening, is, like Sauron, unable to take proper shape again. The first two novels end in his fresh defeat, but he keeps returning. The third book of the series does not feature Voldemort himself. Instead, it introduces the Dementors, grim heirs of the Ringwraiths, who are unable to see properly and can only sense things around them. Although at first they are not directly allied to Voldemort, it becomes clear in the fourth volume that they are his natural servants. Voldemort himself does not lack a finger as Sauron does, but his deputy, Peter Pettigrew, or Scabbers, is missing one. The fourth book shows Voldemort re-embodied, but it remains to be seen how Rowling will work out her final combat.

Many partings

Of course, there have been conscious attempts to break away from the Tolkien mould and to take fantasy in different directions, as the general richness and diversity of the genre shows. Philip Pullman, author of the acclaimed *His Dark Materials* series: *Northern Lights* (1995) (US title: *The Golden Compass*), *The Subtle Knife* (1997) and *The Amber Spyglass* (2000), is a writer who has attempted such a departure. While acknowledging Tolkien's enormous influence on the genre, Pullman has also strongly indicated that he thinks of his own trilogy as having consciously avoided the Tolkien mould of fantasy. His work has no elves, no wizards and no dwarves. It is, as he has said, a work about growing up, but placed within a fantasy setting.

When he wrote *The Fionavar Tapestry*, Kay wanted to show that high fantasy was 'deep enough' to be used originally and in a variety of ways, and that it did not always have to be an imitation of Tolkien. He uses certain elements from Tolkien's work – e.g., the maimed but reviving Dark Lord (Rakoth Maugrim has only one hand), the ubiquitous horse clan, the equally ubiquitous elves, etc. But Kay certainly does things differently here.

One of the most successful 'revisions' of Tolkien's types and figures may be found in the work of the inexhaustibly original Diana Wynne Jones. *Dark Lord of Derkholm* is partly a spoof on fantasy stereotypes, some of which originated with Tolkien. There are wizard guides (one of whom is too young to have a beard of his own and has to wear an artificial

 one), glamorous (or 'hottie') elves, stout dwarves (one named Galadriel) and more. At another level, the book suggests that fantasy is in danger of being debased or low-

ered. This is shown in the way the fantasy world has become nothing but a super-scale theme park, which tourists hack through in order to enjoy the stereotyped fantasy experience. This is set against another fantasy, woven around Derk (the man who is bullied into playing the 'Dark Lord' for the Tours), his family and associates, and the way in which the real 'Dark Lord' – the man who runs the Tours – has to be thrown down. In its own scintillating originality, the book demonstrates that not all fantasy need be derivative.

These are only a few examples of the kinds of influence that Tolkien's work has exerted down the years, and over the genre. It is hard to over-estimate the influence of this great writer, as the next section – which looks at Tolkien's influence beyond the book and over the world at large – will show.

7 ～ A Quiet Little Fellow in a Wide World

When the video and DVD of the first part of *The Lord of the Rings* were released in August 2002, sales rapidly broke all records. On the surface, it might seem that before the film the book hardly existed. But nothing could be further from the truth. *The Lord of the Rings* gathered notice from the start, and continued quietly to gain attention and numbers of readers, not to mention profits for Tolkien, through the fifties. It was, however, only in the sixties that what could be called the 'Tolkien phenomenon' really took off. As mentioned earlier, this had something to do with the exposure that Ace's cheap, unauthorised edition of the book had achieved, and the subsequent minor 'furore' over getting people to stop buying the unauthorised edition, which had added 'publicity value'. Another factor that may have played a part in the increase in Tolkien's status was the 'hippie' era. It was around this time that people began to become acutely aware of man's impact on the environment and, to many, Tolkien appeared to be extolling a back-to-nature attitude. In the United States, there were other issues that had begun to reach boiling point and, to some, Tolkien's writing seemed to act as a focal point for these reactions. This was the time of the Vietnam War (and the demonstrations against it) and some people read *The Lord of the Rings* as an anti-war book.

Tolkien societies started springing up like mushrooms (which would have pleased the hobbits) overnight. The Tolkien Society (UK) was founded in 1969 by Vera Chapman and continues to flourish. They issue an annual journal named after the trees of Lothlórien, *Mallorn*, as well as a bi-monthly newsletter, *Amon Hen*. Their website, which can be accessed at http://www.tolkiensociety.org/, is a gateway to a number of websites dedicated to Tolkien and his work, many of which have been created since the recent film.

The Tolkien Society of America, begun by Richard Plotz in 1965, was later absorbed into the Mythopoeic Society in 1972. It did not last long in its original form, but the society was energetic and enthusiastic. Although essentially a society for the converted (some members even spoke Quenya among themselves), it helped to create new fans as well. In

1965, its members wrote to Tolkien, asking whether he would become a member and asking his permission to name themselves out of his books. His reply was amused and friendly. He demurred a little about becoming a member of a society 'inspired by liking for [his] works' and devoted to study and criticism of them (*Letters*, p. 359). He was, however, as he said, quite happy to be associated with them informally. Although he did not directly refuse them permission to use names from *The Lord of the Rings*, he did suggest that it might be more fun to create titles such as the Member for such-and-such-a-place in the Shire. He himself, he said, would be happy to be known as Member for Longbottom. If they insisted on a title of greater dignity, then he thought Member for Michel Delving might be suitable.

With the growing popularity of *The Lord of the Rings*, the work was bound to make its way into other media. People started setting the lyrics to music – the best known of these songs being Donald Swann's *The Road Goes Ever On*. This was played at the Tolkiens' Golden Anniversary Party, with the composer at the piano and a William Elvin (whose name pleased Tolkien) singing the songs.

People began to write parodies too, confident that the work was well-enough known for the jokes to be understood. The best-known parody was *Bored of the Rings* (1969), the Harvard Lampoon written by students at Harvard. Another parody, which has recently sneaked its way round the world via the Internet, is a take-off of the book and the film. The 'Secret Diaries of the Fellowship of the Ring' by 'Cassandra Claire' is written in the style of *Bridget Jones's Diary*. At the time of writing, it can be found at http://www.cynicsteaparty.com/, from which there is a link. They are very funny, though in rather dubious taste.

Don't be precise ... and don't worry

Offers to make a film from the book began to come in soon after its publication. Tolkien and Unwin decided between them that they would accept a film offer only if it provided either 'a respectable treatment of the work, or else large amounts of money'. In 1957, M.G. Zimmerman submitted a script to Tolkien. It failed to meet with his approval, since neither was it true to his work, nor was the amount of money offered sufficient to seduce.

Disney was a possibility, but Tolkien disliked Disney's work. A letter dated as far back as 1937 expresses his 'heartfelt loathing' for Disney productions (*Letters*, p. 17). Twenty years on, he was still expressing distaste for the studio's 'vulgarity'. *World of the Rings*, a book which describes the attempts to put *The Lord of the Rings* into film, comments that Disney's 'wholesome' (mom and apple-pie) image might have caused some problems when it came to portraying the darker aspects of *The Lord of the Rings*. Evil in Disney tends to be rather toned-down and bland, and the 'cutesy' treatment of Merlin in *The Sword in the Stone* might have made Tolkien nervous at the thought of what the Disney animators could do to Gandalf. United Artists bought the film rights in 1969, but, for various reasons, the project was never completed.

In the event, it was *The Hobbit* which first made it to the cinema. This was in an animated version produced in 1977 by Arthur Rankin using a Japanese animation team. Whatever the merits of the production, animation was probably the wrong medium. The strength of Tolkien's world depends on its 'realism', and animation takes that away, flattening and reducing the work (whether *The Hobbit* or *The Lord of the Rings*) by drawing attention to its unreality.

The Lord of the Rings followed *The Hobbit* into animation in 1979. This version has found its way back into outlets retailing videos and DVDs. It was probably thought that in the present mood for 'things Tolkienian', this Ralph Bakshi film-version of the story would be bound to do not-too-badly (especially as it takes it half a volume further than the current film). At the time of its release there was a good deal of hype about the new methods which had been used in its making. These included rotoscoping, a process in which animation is overlaid onto real action sequences, a technique supposed to aid in producing greater realism.

The film, which is reasonably faithful to the text, might have worked. One of its scriptwriters was Peter S. Beagle, himself a well-known writer of fantasy, and among those doing the voices was John Hurt. The rest of the cast list was respectable, if not as famous. However, its producers ran out of money and the film screeched to an abrupt halt at the battle of Helm's Deep, 'ending' with the misleading announcement that the 'forces of darkness [were] driven forever' from Middle-earth. The frustration caused by this 'ending' cannot be understated.

The recent film, starring Sir Ian McKellen and Elijah Wood, has avoided the problems of animation. The film has many strengths. There is breathtaking scenery, a visual realisation of Tolkien's Middle-earth which few would complain about (it was realised with the help of two of the best-known Tolkien illustrators, John Howe and Alan Lee), and, by and large, an impressive cast. The purists, however (among whom the author is numbered), complain about the cutting of certain sections, e.g. the sequence involving the Barrow-wights, that with Farmer Maggot, the gifting of the Fellowship other than that of Bilbo. They complain even more about the film's inclusion of Arwen. In the book, Arwen is a minor character, but the film gives her some of Frodo's best lines – lines which are quite important in establishing his rejection of Sauron, even in his weakened state. There are also some problems with interpretation, which irritate Tolkien devotees, but the huge success of the film has ensured Tolkien's continuing popularity with a new audience.

The Tolkien phenomenon continues, and it seems unlikely to decrease in the foreseeable future. The current film, and its producer's ploy of releasing it in sections, is likely to see to that for a while. It has been reported that sales of Tolkien's novel, always high, have seen an increase of 600% since the release of the first part of the film. But even when (or if) the film's impact dies down, *The Lord of the Rings* will remain one of the greatest books of the last century.

Appendix A: A Short History of Middle-earth

*Note: FA denotes the First Age, SA the Second Age and TA the Third Age.

First Age

Sauron's involvement in the history of Middle-earth began early. Sauron, who was a Maia (one of the lesser Ainur or angelic beings), became Melkor's lieutenant. Melkor himself had once been the wisest and most powerful of the Ainur, but he had been corrupted by his desire for power. He fled to Middle-earth, which he tried to rule. Melkor then became known as Morgoth. This was during the First Age.

In FA 466, Sauron captured Beren, whom he kept in his pits, till Lúthien and the great hound Huan came to rescue him. It had been foretold that Huan would die fighting the greatest wolf in Arda (Earth). Sauron wanted to bring the prophecy to pass and took the shape of a wolf. He fought with Huan, but was defeated. Yielding mastery of his tower to Lúthien, he then took the shape of a vampire in which he fled to Taur-na-Fuin. He was dormant for the rest of the First Age.

Second Age

After Morgoth fell and was flung out into the Void, Sauron at first submitted himself to justice. He may truly have repented, but perhaps feared that his punishment would be a long period of slavery, and was unable to face the humiliation. He fled and hid himself in Middle-earth, where he fell back into evil. His rise to power began again at about 500 in the Second Age. He took Mordor as his domain, and there he began building the Barad-dûr in SA 1000. Sauron then began plotting to gain ever-greater power over Middle-earth. Making friends with Men and with the Elves, he hid his dark designs and put on a fair-seeming face. He took the name of 'Annatar', which meant 'Lord of Gifts', and passed on his knowledge of crafting. Only Elrond and Gil-galad, the Elven high-king, distrusted him, although they did not yet know who he really was.

During the Second Age, the Elves established a kingdom in Eregion, which was near the great dwarf halls of Khazad-dûm under the mountains. Khazad-dûm became known as Moria after the Balrog who had been hiding there was uncovered and killed two of the dwarf Kings. There was at this time great friendship between the dwarves of Khazad-dûm and the Elves in Eregion, and both races – one skilled in mining, the other in crafting – prospered from the contact.

The greatest of the Elf jewel-smiths was Celebrimbor. He was deceived by Sauron and helped him to forge the rings of power. This happened in SA 1500. The three Elven Rings, Narya, Nenya and Vilya, were forged by Celebrimbor alone. Sauron

forged the One Ring, which he designed so that it would have power over all the other rings of power. However, the moment that Sauron put it on, his designs became clear and the Elves hid the three rings and did not use them.

The War of the Elves and Sauron (SA 1693–1701) began as a result of Sauron's treachery over the rings. Eregion was laid waste. It was at this time that Imladris, or Rivendell, was set up by Elrond as an Elven refuge. The nine rings that Sauron had given to Men corrupted them, turning them into Ringwraiths. They became slaves to Sauron and were his most terrible servants. Sauron then became known as the Dark

Lord and the Enemy, and his reach spread ever farther.

The years SA 1000–3441 are known as the Dark or Black Years. They were the years of Sauron's greatest power in Middle-earth. During these years, Sauron suffered temporary setbacks, but it was not until the Last Alliance of Men and Elves that he was overthrown. One of these setbacks came at the hands of the Númenoreans, who were Elf-friends and a great race of Men. They had been granted Númenor and given many gifts for their faithfulness to the Eldar in the War of the Jewels. (The full account of this may be found in *The Silmarillion*.) They were great mariners, and when they first came to Middle-earth, they had passed on their skills. Although not immortal, they had lifespans longer than those of ordinary men.

By the time of the Black Years, however, the Númenoreans had begun to decline. They had grown proud and discontented. Many of them spoke against the Valar and the Ban, which prevented them from sailing to the Undying Lands. Some of them mistakenly thought that if they went there, they would gain the immortality they desired. The King of Númenor, Ar-Pharazôn, whose abandoned Elvish name had been Tar-Calion, was particularly proud and ambitious. In SA 3362, when Sauron took the title 'King of Men', he responded by landing at Umbar and taking Sauron hostage, carrying him back to Númenor.

Sauron remained in Númenor for fifty years and, while there, further corrupted the morally decaying court. At his persuasion, the tree Nimloth the Fair was cut down and a temple to Melkor built. He persuaded Ar-Pharazôn to rebel against the Valar, and the Númenorean king sent a fleet to Aman. In SA 3319, the Valar's response was to take the Undying Lands out of the world. This was called the Change of the World, and in that Change new continents were formed and Númenor was destroyed, sinking below the waves, like Atlantis. Sauron was caught up in the destruction of Númenor and was so damaged that he was never again able to assume a fair form. He fled back to Middle-earth, where he found that Gil-galad's power had grown greatly in his absence.

Elendil the Tall and his sons Isildur and Anárion had escaped from the destruction of Númenor. They took with them the Seven Seeing Stones – the Palantíri – and the White Tree, which had grown from a fruit of Nimloth. Their ship was blown to Middle-earth, where Elendil met and made friends with Gil-galad. Elendil established the kingdoms of Gondor and Arnor in SA 3320, and became their first high king. The great cities of Osgiliath, Minas Ithil and Minas Tirith were established, and Isengard was also built by men of Númenorean blood.

In SA 3429, Sauron took the war to Gondor and captured Minas Ithil, which was subsequently renamed Minas Morgul by the Gondoreans. He also destroyed the White Tree. Elendil and Gil-galad were determined to move against Sauron, and forged the Last Alliance of Men and Elves. Sauron was defeated at the Battle of Dagorlad (SA 3434) and besieged in the Barad-dûr. A battle in SA 3441 dealt a final defeat to Sauron, but also left Gil-galad and Elendil dead on the slopes of Mount Doom. Elendil's sword, Narsil, was broken, but Isildur took up its hilt and cut the One Ring from Sauron's hand. Sauron's spirit fled his body to hide in the waste places and did not take shape again for many years.

Third Age

With the defeat of Sauron, the Second Age drew to a close and the Third Age began. In this Age, Men and Elves drew apart. Isildur refused to heed the advice of Elrond, who had counselled destroying the One Ring in Mount Doom. He claimed the ring for himself in compensation for the deaths of his father and brother. Isildur, however, was ambushed by Orcs on his way to Eriador, jumped into the river and put on the Ring in an attempt to escape. As he was swimming, the Ring fell off and Isildur was shot by the Orcs (TA 2). Isildur's family were also killed, all except his wife and youngest son, Valandil, who had been left in Rivendell; it was from him that Aragorn was descended. The shards of Narsil were returned to Valandil by Isildur's squire, Ohtar, who had also survived.

In Middle-earth, few of Númenorean descent had survived the war with Sauron in the Second Age, and the kingdoms of Gondor and Arnor began to decline. The Men of Westernesse, or the Dúnedain of the North, as they were known, became a 'strange people wandering secretly in the wild'. For a time, Gondor continued to prosper, but eventually it too began to diminish. The Great Plague of TA 1636–7 was in part responsible for this: it devastated Osgiliath, whose population shrank drastically. In TA 1640, it was abandoned as the capital in favour of Minas Tirith. The plague also killed the king and his family. After the plague, the forts on the borders of Mordor were abandoned. This allowed evil to enter again into Mordor, when the Ringwraiths secretly used the forts to prepare for Sauron's return.

The direct line of kings descended from Isildur's brother, Anárion, finally failed in TA 2050. King Ondoher, the thirty-first king of Gondor, and both his sons had been killed in battle in TA 1944, and the

crown was given to Eärnil, who had been Captain of the Southern Army and was also descended from Anárion. His son, Eärnur, was the last king of the line of Anárion. In riding to Minas Morgul, where he had gone in response to a challenge by the Lord of the Nazgûl, Eärnur rode to his death. When he failed to return, the line of Ruling Stewards held and ruled the City in trust for the king, awaiting his return. Not all the Ruling Stewards believed that a king would reign again in Gondor, nor did they all agree that the line of Isildur had a right to its kingship.

The Third Age saw the Istari appear in Middle-earth. The Istari, or the Wizards, were of the Maiar. Like Sauron and the Balrogs, they were lesser angelic beings. There were five Istari: Saruman the White, Gandalf the Grey (later the White), Radagast the Brown, and two others who are not named in the histories. It was said that they had been sent by the Valar to Middle-earth to contest the power of Sauron, should that ever again become necessary.

The Shadow began to rise and take shape again. Sauron established himself as the Necromancer of Dol Guldur, and Gandalf, at great risk, set out to discover the identity of the Necromancer. The White Council met to discuss ways of dealing with Sauron, but Saruman counselled that they should wait. He claimed that the One Ring had passed away from Middle-earth. However, he desired to find the ring and keep it for himself. A second meeting of the White Council urged action before Sauron's power grew unshakeable. This resulted in their assailing Sauron in Dol Guldur. Although they succeeded in driving him out, they could do no more than this. Sauron took up residence again in Mordor.

The subsequent history of the Third Age, and the War of the Ring which followed, are recounted in *The Lord of the Rings*.

Appendix B: A Who's Who of Middle-earth

Appendices B, C and D contain a brief guide to the key characters and events of Middle-earth. The list is far from exhaustive, but presents a selection of the characters, places and things to be found in Middle-earth. It is designed for use as a quick reference guide to those who have been mentioned in the main body of this book, as well as a few others.

Ainur (singular: Ainu) Holy ones/angelic beings of Illúvatar (God). Of these, there are the greater Ainur, among which fall the Valar (the fourteen greatest Ainur, excluding Melkor), and the Maiar (singular: Maia), the lesser Ainur, which category includes the Istari, Sauron and the Balrogs.

Ancalagon the Black (**Dragon**) Greatest of the winged dragons; killed by Eärendil.

Aragorn (**Man**) Son of Arathorn, descendant of Isildur and, as such, heir to Gondor. Also known as 'Strider' and 'Elessar'. Aragorn is betrothed, and later married, to Arwen Evenstar, daughter of Elrond. He is of the blood of the ancient Númenoreans, who had a lifespan much greater than that of ordinary men, and although this has, by the time of Aragorn, dwindled, Aragorn himself still has a lifespan of about 210 years. Until his ascension, he was Chief of the Dúnedain or Rangers of the North. After Gandalf's 'fall' in Moria, Aragorn assumes leadership of the Fellowship of the Ring, guiding them out of Moria and on to Lothlórien. When the Fellowship breaks up, he takes Gimli and Legolas on a hunt for the Orcs, who have hobbit-napped Merry and Pippin, but failing to find them, joins with the Rohirrim and Ents to fight Saruman. He then takes the Paths of the Dead, and arrives at the battle on the fields of the Pelennor to fight at Éomer's side. He is active at the siege of Gondor, and first manifests his healing abilities ('the hands of the king are the hands of a healer') with Faramir, Éowyn and Merry in the Houses of Healing. Aragorn assumes kingship of the Reunited Kingdom after the War of the Ring is successfully concluded, using the name 'Elessar'. His house is called 'Telcontar', which means 'Strider' in Quenya.

Ar-Pharazôn (Man) Last king of Númenor. Proud and arrogant, he is affronted by Sauron's claiming the title 'King of Men', and takes Sauron hostage, bringing him to Númenor. Listening to Sauron's evil advice, he brings a fleet to the Undying Lands, which were forbidden to the Númenoreans. As a result, the Undying Lands are removed from Arda, and in the resulting Change of the World, Númenor is destroyed.

Arwen (Elven) Also called Undómiel or Evenstar. Daughter of Elrond and Celebrían and grand-daughter of Celeborn and Galadriel. Betrothed, later wife, of Aragorn. Chooses not to go over the Sea, but to take the path of Mortals and die.

Balin (Dwarf) Son of Fundin. Of the House of Durin, and follower of Thráin, and later his son, Thorin. Part of the expedition to the Lonely Mountain to reclaim the treasure from Smaug. He sets up a dwarf colony in Khazad-dûm, but is shot by an Orc in Dimrill Dale. His tomb is in Moria.

Balrogs (Maiar) These were Maiar who joined Melkor in his rebellion and fell with him. Effectively, fallen angels. They were among the most terrible and powerful of Melkor's servants, being spirits of fire and bearing whips of flame.

Bard (Man) Descendant of Girion of Dale and notable archer. He kills Smaug during the dragon's attack on Esgaroth, leads the Men in the Battle of the Five Armies, and uses his share of the dragon hoard to rebuild Dale, of which he subsequently becomes king.

Beorn Skin-changer who often takes the shape of a bear. He shows hospitality to Gandalf, the Dwarves and Bilbo on their trip to the Lonely Mountain.

Beren (Man) Man of the First Age; Elf-friend. Joined outlaws of Dorthonian for a time, but fell in love with the Elf Lúthien, whom he saw dancing in Neldoreth. The price her father Thingol demanded for agreeing to their marriage was a Silmaril. At that time, Morgoth held all three of the Jewels. Beren was captured by Sauron, but escaped with the help of Lúthien and Huan the great hound. He took a Silmaril from the Iron Crown, but in the retreat had a hand bitten off by Carcharoth, the wolf guarding Angband. Beren died, but he and Lúthien were given second lives by the Valar. Beren and Lúthien were the ancestors of Elrond.

Bilbo Baggins (Hobbit) Son of Bungo Baggins and Belladonna Took. Accompanies Gandalf, Thorin and company to the Lonely Mountain as their hired burglar. On the way, he acquires Sting and finds the Ring while wandering in the tunnels after being captured by the goblins. He refrains from killing Gollum, who had formerly possessed the Ring. It is he who discovers the weak point of Smaug the dragon, which allows Smaug to be killed by Bard's arrow. Passes the Ring on to Frodo before leaving for Rivendell on his eleventy-first birthday. Bilbo leaves with Frodo and the Keepers of the Elven Rings to go over the Sea at the ending of the Third Age.

Boromir (Man) Elder son of Denethor, Steward of Gondor. Member of the Fellowship of the Ring. His attempt to take the Ring from Frodo causes the breaking of the Fellowship, since it prompts Frodo and Sam to strike out for Mordor on their own. Dies at the hands of the Orcs in defence of Pippin and Merry and his body is sent, along with the broken Horn of Gondor, over the Falls of Rauros.

Celeborn (Elven) Lord of the Galadhrim (Silvan Elves) in Lothlórien. Husband of Galadriel.

Celebrimbor (Elven) Greatest of the Elven craftsmen in Middle-earth during the Second Age. He was the maker of the three Elven Rings, Nenya, Narya and Vilya, and, unaware of Sauron's intentions, helped him to forge the other rings of power. When Sauron forged the One Ring and his designs became clear, Celebrimbor hid the three Elven Rings. He was killed during the following war between Sauron and the Elves.

Denethor (Man) Last Ruling Steward of Gondor. Father of Boromir and Faramir. Falls into despair, deceived by the lies of Sauron, and dies by his own hand during the Siege of Gondor.

Eärendil (Elven) Father of Elrond. His petition to the Valar moves them to intervene in the wars between Morgoth and the Eldar, resulting in Morgoth's being thrown out into the Timeless Void.

Eärnil (Man) Eärnur's father. Captain of the Southern Army of Gondor, who is given the throne of Gondor on the death of Ondoher and his two sons in battle.

Eärnur (Man) Last King of Gondor of the line of Anárion. He dies (or is presumed to have died) as a result of taking up a challenge to meet the Lord of the Nazgûl in single combat in Minas Morgul. Eärnur never marries and leaves no heirs.

Elendil (Man) Dúnadan of Númenor, first High King of Gondor and Arnor. Father of Isildur. Joins the Last Alliance of Men and Elves, but dies in battle on the slopes of Mount Doom. His son cuts the Ring from

Sauron's hand and claims it as weregild, or compensation, for the deaths of his father and brother.

Elrond (Half-Elven) Son of Eärendil and Elwing, and father of Arwen. Master of Rivendell and Keeper of the Ring Vilya. Is the standard-bearer of the forces of the Last Alliance of Men and Elves in the war against Sauron in the Second Age. His advice that Isildur destroy the Ring goes unheeded. At the end of the Third Age, Elrond departs over the Sea.

Elves and half-Elves Also called the Eldar.

Éomer (Man) Nephew of Théoden and brother of Éowyn. Becomes King of the Mark on Théoden's death. Fights at the Battle of Helm's Deep against the forces of Saruman, and rides to Gondor with the Rohirrim to aid in its defence. After the War of the Ring, Éomer marries Lothíriel, daughter of Imrahil, Prince of Dol Amroth.

Éowyn (Man) Sister of Éomer and niece of Théoden. Falls in love with Aragorn, but this not being reciprocated, rides in disguise to Gondor to seek her death in battle. She fells the Lord of the Nazgûl, and lies near death in the Houses of Healing until healed by Aragorn. Subsequently marries Faramir, Prince of Ithilien.

Faramir (Man) Second son of Denethor, Steward of Gondor. Captain of the Rangers in Ithilien, and leader of the retreat from Osgiliath. He is wounded and falls under the Black Breath and, although nearly burned alive by his suicidal father, is saved by the efforts of Pippin, Beregond and Gandalf, to lie in the Houses of Healing until Aragorn comes to heal him. Subsequently becomes Prince of Ithilien and marries Éowyn.

Frodo Baggins (Hobbit) Nephew of Bilbo, and adopted by him. Is given the Ring by Bilbo, and keeps it for many years before the coming of the Black Riders causes him to leave for Rivendell. At the Council of Elrond, he volunteers to carry the Ring to Mordor and attempt to destroy it in Mount Doom; the Fellowship of the Ring is formed. When Boromir tries to take the Ring from him, Frodo, accompanied by Sam, decides to leave the Fellowship and go on by himself. On the way, they capture Gollum, but Frodo, in remembrance of Bilbo's earlier mercy to Gollum, also refrains from killing him. Frodo's kindness succeeds in taming Gollum, but not totally. On reaching Mount Doom, Frodo, on whom the evil of the Ring has been at work, decides not to destroy the Ring, but to put it on and assume its power. Gollum, however, bites off his finger bearing the Ring and falls into Mount Doom. Frodo, who becomes known in song as Frodo of the Nine Fingers, returns to the Shire, but is never totally healed of the pain, both physical and psychological, that his experiences have brought him. At the end of the Third Age, he leaves to go over the Sea.

Galadriel (Elven) Wife of Celeborn, and Lady of Lothlórien. Princess of the Noldorin branch of the Eldar, whose rebellion against the Valar first brought them to Middle-earth. (See *Silmarillion*.) Keeper of the Ring Nenya, Galadriel departs over the Sea with the other Keepers and Ring-bearers at the end of the Third Age.

Gandalf the Grey, later Gandalf the White (Istar) Next to Saruman, most powerful of the Istari, or Wizards. Known as Mithrandir to the Elves, Keeper of Narya, one of the Elven Rings, and rider of Shadowfax. Most of what we know about Gandalf concerns his doings in the Third Age, during which events in *The Hobbit* and *The Lord of the Rings* are set. Gandalf was responsible for advertising Bilbo as a burglar and getting him hired by Thorin and his twelve companions. He accompanies them, effectively in the role of guide and protector, for part of their journey to the Lonely Mountain, rescuing them from trolls, goblins and Wargs. Leaving them at Mirkwood, he returns at the Battle of the Five Armies. In *The Lord of the Rings*, his probings discover the origin of the Ring. Going to Saruman, the head of his order, he is imprisoned in Orthanc, but escapes with the help of Gwaihir the Windlord. He is part of the Fellowship of the Ring, acting as its leader until his 'fall' in the Mines of Moria from the Bridge of Khazad-dûm in the fight with the Balrog. He is presumed dead, but returns as Gandalf the White and, on Saruman's defeat, takes over as the head of the Istari. Gandalf plays a significant role in the defence of Gondor and after the War of the Ring has been triumphantly concluded, and the Third Age has ended, he leaves Middle-earth to go over the Sea.

Gil-galad (Elven) Elven High-King in the Second Age, part of the Last Alliance of Men and Elves. Defeats Sauron at the Battle of Dagorlad and besieges Barad-dûr, but is killed on the slopes of Mount Doom.

Gimli (Dwarf) Son of Gloin. Member of the Fellowship of the Ring.

Glaurung the Golden (Dragon) Evil dragon created by Morgoth during the First Age, and used by him in the battles against the Elves. Killed by Túrin.

Gollum (Hobbit) Also called Sméagol. Thought to have been a hobbit of the Stoor family, before his murder of his cousin Déagol for the Ring, and his subsequent long hiding underground, turned him into the crawling creature with greenly glowing eyes, which he is for the duration of *The Hobbit* and *The Lord of the Rings*. He plays at riddles with Bilbo, during which he learns the name 'Baggins'. Subsequently, when he emerges to begin looking for the Ring, his 'precious', he is captured by Sauron and tortured, whereupon the surname of Baggins becomes known to Sauron. Gollum follows the Fellowship through Moria, and continues to trail Frodo and Sam after they have left the Fellowship. He is captured by them, and partly tamed, regaining something of his old self, but the lure of the Ring proves too great. At the last, he bites off Frodo's finger with the Ring on it, but topples into the Cracks of Doom, becoming the inadvertent saviour of Middle-earth as the Ring is destroyed.

Gríma Wormtongue (Man) Counsellor to Théoden, and secret traitor to him. Leaves him to throw in his lot with Saruman, whom he later kills in the Shire.

Gwaihir the Windlord King of the Eagles. Rescues

Gandalf from Orthanc, does so for a second time after Gandalf's battle with the Balrog, and flies with other Eagles to rescue Frodo and Sam from Mount Doom after the Ring has been destroyed.

Huan Great Hound, with certain special abilities, probably due to his nature, which had something of the Valar in it. He is untiring, resistant to magic, and thrice in his life uses words to speak. His love for Lúthien causes him to help her in her quest for the Silmaril. He battles Sauron in wolf form, but dies in the fight with Carcharoth, the guardian wolf of Angband.

Ioreth (Man) Oldest of the women in the Houses of Healing, who first recalls the saying that 'the hands of the king are the hands of a healer'.

Isildur (Man) Son of Elendil. Cuts the Ring from Sauron's hand and, rather than destroy it in Mount Doom, decides to keep it as owing to him for his father's death. Is ambushed by Orcs in the Gladden Fields and, by putting on the Ring and jumping into the Anduin, hopes to escape them. The Ring falling off into the river, he is seen and slain by the Orcs. Ancestor of Aragorn.

Legolas (Elven) Elven prince, son of King Thranduil of the Woodland realm. Member of the Fellowship of the Ring.

Lúthien (Elven) Elven princess, daughter of Thingol of Doriath and Melian, one of the Maiar. Beren falls in love with her when he sees her dancing in the moonlight. Her father Thingol opposes their marriage unless Beren can win him a Silmaril. She follows Beren on his quest with Huan the great hound, defeats Sauron to win Beren's release from his pits, and goes with him to Angband to help him win the Silmaril from Morgoth. When Beren dies, Lúthien, who has surrendered her immortality, dies too; the Valar take pity on her and restore both her and Beren to a second life. During this second lifetime, she wears a necklace made by the Dwarves: the Nauglamír, which contains the Silmaril taken from Morgoth.

Maiar Lesser Ainur.

Melkor/Morgoth (Ainu) Once the greatest of the Ainur. Corrupted many of the Maiar, and waged war against the Valar, wanting to claim Arda (Earth) as his own, but was defeated (First War) though Arda was marred in the process. He destroyed the Two

Lamps of the Valar, but in the subsequent Battle with the Valar was again defeated and imprisoned for three ages, although he was eventually released. He stole the Silmarils, his hands being burned by the holy jewels, and he fled to Middle-earth, where he became known as Morgoth, continuing to corrupt whatever he came into contact with. Sauron was his lieutenant in the long war against the Eldar, which was eventually brought to an end through the intervention of the Valar. Morgoth was then cast out into the Timeless Void.

Meriadoc Brandybuck (Hobbit) One of the Fellowship of the Ring. Known mostly as 'Merry'. He and Pippin are captured by Orcs, although defended by Boromir. Escaping by using their wits and through luck, he and Pippin find themselves in Fangorn Forest, where they meet Treebeard and tell him their story, as a result of which the Ents join the war against Saruman. Merry later swears himself to Théoden, and secretly accompanies Éowyn, who is disguised as Dernhelm, to war at Gondor. It is his sword, made by the long-ago men of Westernesse and taken from the Barrow-downs, which is used by him to hamstring the King of the Ringwraiths, causing the Ringwraith to stumble, and giving Éowyn the chance to kill the Ringwraith. He is later healed by Aragorn in the Houses of Healing, and then returns home to help in the Scouring of the Shire.

Ondoher (Man) Thirty-first king of Gondor. Dies in battle against the Wainriders, an Easterling people who had been incited by Sauron to make war on Gondor.

Peregrin Took (Hobbit) Son of Paladin. Known mostly as 'Pippin'. One of the Fellowship of the Ring. With Merry, he is captured by the Orcs, but escapes. They are found by Treebeard, and drink of the Ent draughts, as a result of which they grow taller than hobbits are wont to do, their hair also growing curlier. Insatiably curious, Pippin picks up the Palantír, which Gríma throws out of Orthanc, and is tempted into stealing it. He looks into it, seeing the Eye of Sauron, and is interrogated by him. He is whisked off by Gandalf to Minas Tirith, where he swears fealty to Denethor, becoming a Guard. It is he who, seeing Denethor about to burn himself and his son Faramir, runs to get Beregond and Gandalf. He returns after the war to help in the Scouring of the Shire.

Radagast the Brown (Istar) One of the Istari. Fairly minor figure, whose main role in the action seems to have been to aid in Gandalf's escape (without knowing it), by sending Gwaihir to look for Gandalf. Known to be wise in the matter of herbs and beasts.

Ringwraiths Also known as the Nazgûl. Servants of Sauron 'created' during the Second Age. Originally men corrupted by Sauron's gift of the Nine Rings. The chief of the Ringwraiths is the former Witch-king of Angmar. In the Third Age, when they first set out for the Shire to look for 'Baggins', they are mounted on black steeds, stolen from Rohan, and are called the Black Riders. These steeds, however, are destroyed when the Ringwraiths attempt to cross the Ford of Bruinen (Ford of Rivendell), and the Ringwraiths are remounted by Sauron on winged beasts. The Lord of the Ringwraiths is killed in the battle on the fields of the Pelennor by Éowyn, after being wounded by Merry wielding a weapon made by the ancient men of Westernesse.

Samwise Gamgee (Hobbit) Faithful servant of Frodo. One of the Fellowship of the Ring. Accompanies Frodo when Frodo leaves the rest of the Fellowship. When Frodo is poisoned by Shelob, Samwise carries the Ring for a while, thus becoming, himself, a Ring-bearer for a time. He rescues Frodo from Shelob, and it is his unfailing support for Frodo which finally gets them both to the Crack of Doom. Sam, as he is known, goes back to the Shire after the War is over, and marries Rose Cotton. He, unlike the other Ring-bearers, does not go over the Sea.

Saruman the White (Istar) Also known as Curunír, the 'Man of Skill'. Originally head of the White Council, and at first the most powerful and wise of the Istari. Is, however, corrupted by the desire for power and the Ring and, using the Palantír of Orthanc, is trapped by Sauron and bent to his will. He imprisons Gandalf in Orthanc when Gandalf refuses to aid him. Thrown down after the war with Rohan, he is for a time kept prisoner in Orthanc and guarded by Treebeard, who finally allows him to go free. He makes his way to the Shire to wreak havoc there as 'Sharkey'; on the return of Frodo and his companions, he is deposed and is subsequently murdered by Gríma Wormtongue.

Sauron (Maia) His name means 'abominable' in Quenya. Also called Gorthaur by the Elves. One of the Maiar corrupted by Melkor in the First Age, and later his lieutenant. He falls with Morgoth, but flees and hides somewhere in Middle-earth while his power builds again slowly, eventually establishing a stronghold in Mordor. During the Second Age,

Sauron tricks Celebrimbor into forging the various rings of power, while he himself forges the One Ring, which will control the others. The Battle of Dagorlad, in which he is pitted against the Last Alliance of Men and Elves, sees him defeated; Elendil and Gil-galad are, however, killed in the conflict. Isildur, Elendil's son, cuts off Sauron's finger and takes the Ring, and Sauron is, for a time, left powerless and without shape. He eventually returns as the Necromancer of Dol Guldur, but is then driven out of Dol Guldur by the White Council. He returns to Mordor, and begins to search for the One Ring, while building up his armies of Orcs and Men. His power is finally destroyed when the One Ring falls into Orodruin, and he is unable to take shape ever again.

Smaug the Golden (Dragon) Destroys Dale and takes the treasure of the Kings under the Mountain from the Dwarves there. Killed by Bard during his attack on Esgaroth.

Tar-Calion (Man) see Ar-Pharazôn.

Théoden (Man) King of the Mark and uncle to Éomer and Éowyn. His councillor Gríma's whisperings demoralise and weaken Théoden for a time, but Gandalf comes to put heart back into him. He rides out against Saruman to win the Battle of Helm's Deep, and then leads the Rohirrim to relieve the Siege of Gondor. He slays the Standard Bearer of the hosts of Mordor, but is then himself killed as a result of his horse Snowmane falling on him when she is pierced by a black dart of the King of the Ringwraiths.

Thorin Oakenshield (Dwarf) Leader of the expedition to reclaim the treasure of Smaug. Killed at the Battle of the Five Armies and buried with the Arkenstone and Orcrist.

Treebeard (Ent) Oldest of the Ents. Brings the Ents to war against Saruman and is left to keep an eye on the imprisoned Saruman in Orthanc after the others have left for the siege of Minas Tirith. However, he is persuaded to let Saruman go free.

*Note: Those wishing a more comprehensive guide than the brief notes given here should consult Robert Foster's wonderfully clear *The Complete Guide to Middle-earth*.

Appendix C: A Where's Where of Middle-earth

Barad-dûr The fortress of Sauron built with the power of the One Ring, whose name means 'Dark Tower'.

Bree Town of Men and hobbits, where the Prancing Pony, the Inn kept by Barliman Butterbur, is. It is here that the hobbits first meet Aragorn in the persona of 'Strider'.

Dale City-kingdom of Men, destroyed by Smaug and rebuilt by Bard.

Esgaroth City of Men, located on the Long Lake, supplying Erebor and the Woodland Realm. Destroyed by Smaug, but rebuilt with some of the treasure taken from Smaug's hoard.

Falls of Rauros Waterfalls on the river Anduin, over which the boat bearing the body of Boromir and the Horn of Gondor is sent.

Fangorn Forest Forest at the southern end of the Misty Mountains. Inhabited by Treebeard the Ent, who is also known as Fangorn, and by the other Ents. Trees from Fangorn are chopped down by Saruman to feed the fires of Orthanc.

Gondor Kingdom of Men founded by Elendil. Once powerful, it has degenerated by the time of the War of the Ring. Its chief cities are Minas Anor, Minas Ithil, Dol Amroth and Osgiliath. By the time of the War of the Ring, Osgiliath has been lost, Minas Ithil captured and renamed as Minas Morgul, and Minas Anor has acquired the new name of Minas Tirith. After Elendil is killed, Gondor is ruled by the line of his son, Anárion. When this line fails, Gondor is administered by the Ruling Stewards, a post which descends from father to son, until the return of Aragorn.

Helm's Deep The stronghold from which Westfold, in Rohan, is defended. 'Helm's Deep' refers to the whole system of fortifications in the area, including the fortress the Hornburg. Site of a major battle against the forces of Saruman in which Théoden, Aragorn, Éomer, Legolas and Gimli take part.

Isengard Fortress originally built by Gondor in the days of its power, which is why a Palantír is kept there, though it has been forgotten about. It is held by Saruman until its destruction by the Ents.

Khazad-dûm Greatest of the Dwarf-halls, stretching underneath a good part of the Misty Mountains. Mithril is discovered in the mines here. Khazad-dûm becomes known as Moria (the 'Black Pit') after the Balrog, which the Dwarves have inadvertently freed while mining, kills two of the Dwarf kings. The loosing of the Balrog causes Khazad-dûm to be deserted by the Dwarves, after which it is kept full of Orcs by Sauron. Balin, son of Fundin, later attempts to resettle part of Khazad-dûm, but is killed in Dimrill Dale. When the Fellowship of the Ring passes through Moria, it is attacked by trolls, Orcs and the Balrog. Gandalf fights the Balrog; both fall from the Bridge of Khazad-dûm. The Balrog is finally slain by Gandalf after a prolonged battle. There is no record, however, that Khazad-dûm is ever resettled by the Dwarves.

The Lonely Mountain/Erebor Lying to the east of Mirkwood, which had originally been lived in by many of Durin's Folk, who founded the Kingdom under the Mountain. This is destroyed by Smaug, who has his lair there until he is killed by Bard, after which Dain II re-establishes the Kingdom of the Dwarves under the Mountain.

Lothlórien Elven realm ruled by Celeborn and

Galadriel, which is never marred or touched by Sauron.

Meduseld The palace of the Kings of the Mark, with a roof made of gold.

Minas Morgul/Minas Ithil Minas Ithil, whose name means 'Tower of the Moon', is renamed 'Minas Morgul' – 'Tower of Black Magic' – when it falls to the forces of Sauron during the Third Age. After the War of the Ring, it is inhabited again, and takes back its old name. A Palantír is kept in Minas Ithil, but this is captured and taken to Barad-dûr.

Minas Tirith/Minas Anor City of Gondor, which becomes its capital when Osgiliath's population begins to decline due to plague. It is renamed 'Minas Tirith' when Minas Ithil falls to Sauron. Its original name, 'Minas Anor' means 'Tower of the Sun' to complement 'Minas Ithil', which means 'Tower of the Moon'. A Palantír is kept in Minas Anor/Minas Tirith, and used by its rulers.

Mirkwood Forest near Dol Guldur, which has fallen under its darkness. Its northern part is inhabited by the Elves of the Woodland Realm, one of whom is Legolas. It also houses unpleasant creatures, such as black squirrels, and the spiders encountered by Bilbo and the Dwarves on their way to the Lonely Mountain. The waters of the river that pass through it are perilous to drink; Bombur drinks from them and sinks into an enchanted sleep.

Misty Mountains Mountain chain in Middle-earth originally created by Melkor during the First Age. The mountain range includes Zirak-zigil, the mountain atop which Gandalf and the Balrog fight and from which the latter is thrown down. The Dwarves have their palace/Dwarf-halls of Khazad-dûm under it, but these are later deserted by the Dwarves (see entry on Khazad-dûm above) and then infested by Orcs.

Mordor Realm of Sauron. 'Nuff said.

Moria See Khazad-dûm.

Mount Doom/Orodruin The volcano in which the One Ring was forged and into which it has to be thrown in order to be destroyed.

Orthanc The tower of Saruman in Isengard, built of unbreakable black stone. Its name, in the language of the Rohirrim, means 'cunning mind'. Also known as Mount Fang.

Osgiliath Originally the capital of Gondor before a plague, during the Third Age, and other disasters cause the removal of the royal court to Minas Anor.

Rivendell/Imladris Also known as the Last Homely House of the West. Home of Elrond.

The Shire Land inhabited by hobbits. Technically under the rule of the King but, at the time of the War of the Ring, communication has effectively ceased for so long that the existence of hobbits has largely been forgotten.

Weathertop Hill atop which Frodo and his companions encounter the Black Riders and Frodo is pierced by a Morgul-knife.

Appendix D: A What's What of Middle-earth

Andúril/Narsil Sword of Elendil, which is broken during the battle against Sauron in the Second Age. Isildur uses the hilt to cut the One Ring from Sauron's hand. The shards of Narsil are kept at Imladris; it is foretold that the sword should be remade when the Ring is found again. It is reforged for Aragorn and renamed Andúril. Also known as the Blade that was Broken or the Sword Reforged.

Arkenstone Enormous white jewel, also called the Heart of the Mountain, of great beauty and price, which is found by Thorin's father in Erebor. Subsequently part of Smaug's hoard till found by Bilbo and given by him to Bard and his allies so that they can bargain for their rightfully earned share of the treasure being withheld by Thorin. It is afterwards buried with Thorin.

Glamdring Gandalf's sword. Originally made by the Elves of Gondolin, but finds its way into a troll-hoard, from which Gandalf liberates it. It shines with a blue light whenever Orcs are near. It is one of two paired swords, of which the other is Orcrist.

Lembas Waybread of the Elves.

Mirror of Galadriel Basin in Lothlórien which can show scenes from far away or long ago when filled with water.

Mithril Substance much prized by the Dwarves, and found only in Khazad-dûm. It is also known as 'true silver' or 'Moria silver', and does not tarnish. Mithril is light and can be easily beaten into different shapes, but can be made harder than tempered steel. At the time of the War of the Ring, it is almost priceless, since there is little to be found above ground, the mines having been abandoned.

Morgul-knife Enchanted knife used by the Lord of the Ringwraiths to stab Frodo. A fragment of this works its way towards Frodo's heart and, if it were to succeed in piercing it, Frodo would become as the Ringwraiths.

Narya Ring of Fire. One of the three Elven Rings worn by Gandalf. It bears a red stone.

Nenya Ring of Water. This is worn by Galadriel, and is another of the three Elven Rings. It is of mithril with a white stone.

The One Ring Forged by Sauron in Mount Doom to be the master of the other rings of power. Confers the power of invisibility on its wearer. It is cut off Sauron's finger by Isildur, falls off Isildur's finger into the River Anduin, and is found a long time after by Gollum's cousin, whom Gollum murders for it. It is found by Bilbo Baggins when he is wandering about, lost, in the tunnels of the goblins and he passes it to his nephew Frodo, who is given the task of taking the Ring to Mount Doom and destroying it. On reaching Mount Doom after many hardships, Frodo cannot bring himself to destroy it; the finger that bears it, however, is bitten off by Gollum, and falls with Gollum into the volcano and so is destroyed.

Orcrist Sword made by the Elves of Gondolin, which finds its way into a troll-hoard. It is found by Gandalf and given to Thorin Oakenshield. Orcrist is the mate of Glamdring, Gandalf's sword, and shines with a blue light whenever Orcs are near. It is buried with Thorin and said to shine and so give warning whenever enemies are near.

Palantíri (singular: Palantír) Seeing Stones made of crystal. There were originally seven of these stones, which had been brought by Elendil and his sons in their flight from the destruction of Númenor. The

Palantíri can be used to show to their user things far off in space or even time, and can also be used to communicate with each other. By the time of the War of the Ring, only three remain, one of which is with Sauron, one with Denethor in Gondor, and one in Orthanc.

Silmarils Three Jewels made by Fëanor of the Eldar, which shine with the light of the Two Trees of the Valar. Their full history is told in *The Silmarillion*. They are stolen by Morgoth and taken to Middle-earth. One is taken by Beren from the Iron Crown, but swallowed by Carcharoth the wolf, along with Beren's hand. It is subsequently recovered and set into the Nauglamír, a necklace made by the Dwarves, and worn by Lúthien till her death. Lúthien's Silmaril eventually descends to Elwing, who marries Eärendil. It is by the power of the Silmaril that Elwing and Eärendil later win through to the Undying Lands to ask the help of the Valar in the war against Morgoth. Eärendil binds it to his brow, and its light increases as they sail towards their destination. The Valar inter-cede and Morgoth is thrown out into the Void. The Silmaril is afterwards worn by Eärendil, who, in his ship Vingilot, is set in the oceans of heaven by the Valar as a star reminding all of hope. The other two Silmarils are recovered from the Iron Crown, but torment the two Elves who take them: one throws himself into a fiery abyss, the other flings his into the sea. Of the three Silmarils, therefore, one is left in water, one in fire and one in air.

Sting Bilbo's dagger, which is found in the troll-hoard which yields up Orcrist and Glamdring. Shines with a blue light when Orcs are near. Bilbo gives Sting, along with his mithril armour, to Frodo.

Vilya The mightiest of the three Elven Rings, first worn by Gil-galad, but given by him to Elrond. Vilya is the Ring of Air, of gold set with a sapphire.

Bibliography

Professor David Hawkes once wrote in an introduction that he had thought it best not to encumber his text with footnotes, as that might be a bit like asking the reader to play tennis in chains. It was suggested that, this not being an academic book but one intended for the general reader, the same principle should be observed here. It has seemed to me proper, however, to at least acknowledge generally what could not be acknowledged specifically. I have found a few works to be particularly useful while putting this book together. One is Humphrey Carpenter's biography of Tolkien, which has provided much of the basic material for the section on Tolkien's life; another is his book on the Inklings. His biography of Tolkien remains the standard one for all Tolkien scholars. Another book I have found invaluable is Robert Foster's wonderfully comprehensive *Complete Guide to Middle-earth*, which allowed details and dates to be checked quickly and with confidence. I cannot recommend this highly enough. Tolkien's *Letters*, edited by Carpenter, however, may well be the work that has been most valuable. While these are an incomplete record of a life, as all records must inevitably be, the letters allow the voice of Tolkien to be heard unmediated. The man who emerges from the letters – intelligent and informed, courteous, warm, compassionate, humorous and modest – is one whom I wish I could have known.

References

This list contains not only works that have been consulted or directly cited here, but also works that anyone wishing to pursue further reading might consult. The list of critical work pertaining to Tolkien is, of course, a selection only. The edition of *The Lord of the Rings* used is the HarperCollins Modern Classics edition (2001). Dates where given in square brackets indicate the date of original publication.

A. Tolkien: Primary Works (selected)

Tolkien, J.R.R. 'The Adventures of Tom Bombadil' [1961] in *Tales from the Perilous Realm*, (London: HarperCollins, 1997).

—— 'Farmer Giles of Ham' [1949] in *Tales from the Perilous Realm* (London: HarperCollins, 1997).

—— *The Father Christmas Letters* (ed. Baillie Tolkien) (London: Allen and Unwin, 1975).

—— *The Hobbit* [1937] (London: HarperCollins, 1999).

—— 'Leaf by Niggle' [1945] in *Tales from the Perilous Realm* (London: HarperCollins, 1997).

—— *The Lord of the Rings: Part I: The Fellowship of the Ring* [1954, 1966] (London: HarperCollins, 2001).

—— *The Lord of the Rings: Part II: The Two Towers* [1954, 1966] (London: HarperCollins, 2001).

—— *The Lord of the Rings: Part III: The Return of the King* [1955, 1966] (London: HarperCollins, 2001).

—— *Roverandom* (London: Allen and Unwin, 1998).

—— *The Silmarillion* (London: HarperCollins, 1977).

—— 'Smith of Wootton Major' [1967] in *Tales from the Perilous Realm* (London: HarperCollins, 1997).

—— *Tree and Leaf* (edition including 'The Homecoming of Beorhtnoth') (London: HarperCollins, 2001).

—— *Unfinished Tales* (London: HarperCollins, 1980).

B. Tolkien: Biographies/Biographically related material/Correspondence

Carpenter, Humphrey. *J. R. R. Tolkien: A Biography* (London: Allen and Unwin, 1977).

—— *The Inklings* (London: HarperCollins, 1978).

—— (Ed.) *The Letters of J. R. R. Tolkien* (London: HarperCollins, 1995).

Pearce, Joseph. *Tolkien: Man and Myth* (London: HarperCollins, 1998).

White, Michael. *Tolkien: A Biography* (London: Little, Brown, 2001).

Wynne Jones, Diana. 'Official Autobiography', http://www.leemac.freeserve.co.uk

C. Tolkien: Criticism/Reference

Chance, Jane. *The Lord of the Rings: The Mythology of Power* (rev. edition) (Kentucky: The University Press of Kentucky, 2001).

—— *Tolkien's Art: A Mythology for England* (rev. edition) (Kentucky: The University Press of Kentucky, 2001).

Curry, Patrick. *Defending Middle-earth; Tolkien: Myth and Modernity* (Edinburgh: Floris Books, 1997).

Flieger, Verlyn. *Splintered Light: Logos and Language in Tolkien's World* (Michigan: William B. Eerdmans, 1983).

Foster, Robert. *The Complete Guide to Middle-earth* (London: HarperCollins, 1991).

Giddings, Robert (Ed.). *This Far Land* (London: Vision Press, 1983).

Isaacs, Neil D. and Zimbardo, Rose A. (Eds). *Tolkien and the Critics: Essays on J.R.R. Tolkien's 'The Lord of the Rings'* (Notre Dame, IN: University of Notre Dame Press, 1968).

Kocher, Paul. *Master of Middle-earth: The Achievement of J.R.R. Tolkien* (London: Thames and Hudson, 1973).

Lowson, Iain, Marshall, Keith and O'Brien, Daniel. *World of the Rings* (London: Reynolds and Hearn, 2002).

Manlove, Colin. *Modern Fantasy: Five Studies* (Cambridge: Cambridge University Press, 1975).

—— *Christian Fantasy from 1200 to the Present* (Basingstoke: Macmillan, 1992).

—— *The Fantasy Literature of England* (Basingstoke: Macmillan, 1999).

Moseley, Charles. *J.R.R. Tolkien* (Plymouth: Northcote House, 1997).

Rosebury, Brian. *Tolkien: A Critical Assessment* (Basingstoke: Macmillan, 1992).

Shippey, T.A. *Tolkien: Author of the Century* (London: HarperCollins, 2000).

—— *The Road to Middle-earth* (London: HarperCollins, 1992).

Wynne Jones, Diana. 'The Shape of the Narrative in *The Lord of the Rings*' in *This Far Land* (ed. Robert Giddings) (London: Vision Press, 1983).

D. Tolkien: Art/Painting/Graphic novels

Various artists. *Tolkien's World: Paintings of Middle-earth* (London: HarperCollins, 1992).

Tolkien, J.R.R. *The Hobbit* (illustrated by David Wenzel, adapted by Charles Dixon with Sean Deming) (London: HarperCollins, 1989).

E. Other: Non-fiction

Clute, John and Grant, John (Eds). *The Encyclopedia of Fantasy* (New York: Orbit, 1997).

Haber, Karen (Ed.). *Meditations on Middle-earth* (London: Earthlight, 2002).

Jackson, Rosemary. *Fantasy: The Literature of Subversion* (London: Routledge, 1981).

Lewis, C.S. *All My Road Before Me: The Diary of C.S. Lewis, 1922–27* (ed. Walter Hooper) (New York: Harcourt Brace Jovanovich, c. 1991).

—— *Of This and Other Worlds* (ed. Walter Hooper) (London: Fount, 1966).

—— *The Four Loves* [1960] (New York: Phoenix Press, 1986).

Manguel, Alberto. *The Dictionary of Imaginary Places* (London: Bloomsbury, 1999).

Noel, Ruth S. *The Languages of Tolkien's Middle-earth* (Boston: Houghton Mifflin, 1980).

Sayer, George. *Jack: A Life of C.S. Lewis* (Basingstoke: Macmillan, 1988).

Wynne Jones, Diana. *The Tough Guide to Fantasyland* (London: Vista, 1996).

Fiction

*Note: some of the earlier fantasists mentioned, e.g. E. R. Eddison, Lord Dunsany, etc., have been brought back into print in the superb Gollancz Masterworks series; two lists exist: one for science fiction, and one for fantasy.

Alexander, Lloyd. *The Book of Three* [1964] (London: Fontana/Collins, 1966).

Brooks, Terry. *The Sword of Shannara* (New York: Del Rey, 1977).

Cabell, James Branch. *The Cream of the Jest* [1917] (New York: Ballantine, 1971).

—— *Jurgen* (New York: Robert McBride, 1919).

—— *Domnei* [1920] (New York: Ballantine, 1972).

—— *Figures of Earth* [1921] (New York: Ballantine, 1969).

—— *The Silver Stallion* (New York: Robert McBride, 1926).

Carroll, Lewis. *Alice's Adventures in Wonderland* [1865] (Harmondsworth: Puffin, 1955).

Donaldson, Stephen. *The Illearth War* (Glasgow: Fontana/Collins, 1978).

—— *Lord Foul's Bane* (Glasgow: Fontana/Collins, 1978).

—— *The Power that Preserves* (Glasgow: Fontana/Collins, 1978).

—— *The Wounded Land* (Glasgow: Fontana/Collins, 1980).

—— *The One Tree* (Glasgow: Fontana/Collins, 1982).

—— *White Gold Wielder* (Glasgow: Fontana/Collins, 1983).

Dunsany, Lord. *The King of Elfland's Daughter* [1924] (London: Gollancz, 2001).

Eddison, E.R. *The Worm Ouroboros* [1922] (London: Gollancz, 2000).

—— *Mistress of Mistresses* [1935] (London: Gollancz, 2001).

—— *A Fish Dinner in Memison* (New York: E.P. Dutton, 1941).

—— *The Mezentian Gate* (incomplete) (London: Elek Books, 1958).

Edghill, Rosemary. *The Sword of Maiden's Tears* (New York: Daw Books, 1995).

—— *The Cup of Morning Shadows* (New York: Daw Books, 1996).

—— *The Cloak of Night and Daggers* (New York: Daw Books, 1997).

Feist, Raymond. *Magician* (New York: Doubleday, 1982).

—— *Silverthorn* (New York: Doubleday, 1985).

—— *A Darkness at Sethanon* (New York: Doubleday, 1986).

Garner, Alan. *The Weirdstone of Brisingamen*

(London: William Collins, 1960).

Hambly, Barbara. *The Time of the Dark* (New York: Del Rey, 1982).

—— *The Armies of Daylight* (New York: Del Rey, 1983).

—— *The Walls of Air* (New York: Del Rey, 1983).

Kay, Guy Gavriel, *The Darkest Road* (Toronto: Collins, 1984).

—— *The Summer Tree* (Toronto: Collins, 1986).

—— *The Wandering Fire* (Toronto: Collins, 1986).

Le Guin, Ursula. *A Wizard of Earthsea* (California: Parnassus Press, 1968).

—— *The Tombs of Atuan* (New York: Atheneum, 1971).

—— *The Farthest Shore* (New York: Atheneum, 1972).

—— *Tehanu* (New York: Atheneum, 1990).

—— *The Other Wind* (New York: Harcourt Brace, 2001).

Lewis, C.S. *Out of the Silent Planet* (London: The Bodley Head, 1938).

—— *Perelandra* (London: The Bodley Head, 1943).

—— *That Hideous Strength* (London: The Bodley Head, 1945).

—— *The Lion, the Witch and the Wardrobe* (London: The Bodley Head, 1950).

—— *Prince Caspian* (London: The Bodley Head, 1951).

—— *The Voyage of the Dawn Treader* (London: The Bodley Head, 1952).

—— *The Silver Chair* (London: The Bodley Head, 1953).

—— *The Horse and His Boy* (London: The Bodley Head, 1954).

—— *The Magician's Nephew* (London: The Bodley Head, 1955).

—— *Till We Have Faces* (London: Collins, 1956).

—— *The Last Battle* (London: The Bodley Head, 1965).

MacDonald, George. *The Princess and the Goblin* [1872] (Harmondsworth: Puffin, 1964).

—— *The Princess and Curdie* [1882] (Harmondsworth: Puffin, 1966).

Peake, Mervyn. *Titus Groan* (London: Eyre and Spottiswode, 1946).

—— *Gormenghast* (London: Eyre and Spottiswode, 1950).

—— *Titus Alone* (London: Eyre and Spottiswode, 1959).

Rowling, J.K. *Harry Potter and the Philosopher's Stone* (London: Bloomsbury, 1997).

—— *Harry Potter and the Chamber of Secrets* (London: Bloomsbury, 1998).

—— *Harry Potter and the Prisoner of Azkaban* (London: Bloomsbury, 1999).

—— *Harry Potter and the Goblet of Fire* (London: Bloomsbury, 2000).

Siegel, Jan. *Prospero's Children* (London: Voyager, 1999).

Wynne Jones, Diana. *Dark Lord of Derkholm* (London: Gollancz, 1998).

About the Author

Dr Susan Ang is the author of *The Widening World of Children's Literature* (Basingstoke: Macmillan, 2000). She has also contributed articles on children's literature to *Encarta* and *The Cambridge Guide to Children's Books in English* (ed. Victor Watson) (Cambridge: Cambridge University Press, 2002), among which are entries on Tolkien, C.S. Lewis, *The Hobbit* and *The Chronicles of Narnia*. Dr Ang is a lecturer with the Department of English Language and Literature, National University of Singapore, whose teaching lies mainly in the areas of nineteenth-century literature, science fiction and gothic.

Index